ICB Bookkeeping Level III

Advanced Bookkeeping

Kit

KAPLAN
PUBLISHING

British Library Cataloguing-in-Publication Data

A catalogue record for this book is available from the British Library.

Published by:
Kaplan Publishing UK
Unit 2 The Business Centre
Molly Millars Lane
Wokingham
RG41 2QZ

ISBN 978-1-84710-931-6

© Kaplan Financial Limited, 2009
Printed in the UK by CPI William Clowes Beccles NR34 7TL
All rights reserved. No part of this publication may be reproduced, stored in a retrieval system, or transmitted, in any form or by any means, electronic, mechanical, photocopying, recording or otherwise, without the prior written permission of Kaplan Publishing.

The text in this material and any others made available by any Kaplan Group company does not amount to advice on a particular matter and should not be taken as such. No reliance should be placed on the content as the basis for any investment or other decision or in connection with any advice given to third parties. Please consult your appropriate professional adviser as necessary. Kaplan Publishing Limited and all other Kaplan group companies expressly disclaim all liability to any person in respect of any losses or other claims, whether direct, indirect, incidental, consequential or otherwise arising in relation to the use of such materials.

KEY TECHNIQUES QUESTION BANK
Preface   4

Topic	*Questions pg*	*Answers pg*
Accruals and prepayments		
Question 1	7	53
Question 2	9	54
Question 3	10	56
Question 4	11	57
Depreciation		
Question 5	12	58
Question 6	13	60
Question 7	14	62
Question 8	15	63
Trial balance adjustments		
Question 9	16	65
Question 10	17	66
Question 11	18	68
Incomplete records		
Question 12	19	69
Question 13	20	72
Question 14	21	74
Preparing financial statements		
Question 15	22	75
Question 16	24	77
Partnership accounts		
Question 17	26	80
Question 18	28	83
Question 19	30	86
Question 20	32	89
Financial statements for Ltd Companies		
Question 21	34	92
Question 22	36	95
Question 23	38	98
Question 24	40	102
Question 25	42	106
Question 26	44	109
Ratios		
Question 27	46	112
Question 28	47	114
Question 29	48	116
Sample past exam paper	117	121

Revision Kit Preface
This kit has been written for level III of the Institute of Certified Bookkeepers (ICB) Manual route syllabus.

It is designed to compliment the corresponding ICB study text (Advanced Bookkeeping) which contains the detailed syllabus coverage.

The past examination paper has kindly been supplied direct from the Institute of Certified Bookkeepers.

Key Technique Questions

QUESTION 1

GAS, ELECTRICITY AND RENT

(a) A company powers some of its machinery by gas. Accounts are prepared to the 30 June each year. On 1 July 20X5 there was an accrual brought down in the gas account of £650. Bills were received as follows:

Invoice date	Amount £	Quarter end to which bill relates
15.9.20X5	1,200	31.8.20X5
14.12.20X5	1,750	30.11.20X5
18.3.20X6	1,695	28.2.20X6
14.6.20X6	1,560	31.5.20X6

At 30 June 20X6 a reading was taken of the gas meter and an estimated charge for the month of June was computed at £480.

Required:

Write up a ledger account for gas and show the transfer to the profit and loss account.

(7 marks)

(b) The electricity account for A Trader for the year ended 31 December 20X7 appears in the nominal ledger as:

Electricity account

20X7		£		£
8 Mar	Purchases day book	120		
7 Jun	Purchases day book	96		
10 Sep	Purchases day book	72		
8 Dec	Purchases day book	108		
		396		

The bill received after the year end is shown below:

Southern Electric				
Our Service Address is: 14 Broad Road, Hendon, London, H5 6GF				You can contact us on: Tel: 020 8623 0991 Fax: 020 8665 8761
				1220 9/3/20X8
A Trader 22 Boundary Road London H14 5ON				
Meter reading		Units used	Unit price	Amount £
Present	Previous			
E 144202	C 143140	1062	9.51p	101.00
Standing charge		1/12/X7 TO 28/02/X8		25.00
				126.00
		VAT at 17½ %		22.05
Payment due by 15 Mar 20X8 VAT Reg No. 431 3363 81				148.05

Required:

How much should be estimated as being the charge for electricity consumed in December? What would thus be the expense for the year? **(4 marks)**

(c) A business received rental income of £2,000, relating to the six months to 31 March 20X4, on 30 June 20X4. At its year end of 30 September 20X4 the next six-monthly rental of £1,500 had not been received.

Required:

Write up the ledger account for rental income for the year ended 30 September 20X4.

(4 marks)

(Total: 15 marks)

QUESTION 2

XY

At 1 October 20X5, the following balances were brought forward in the ledger accounts of XY:

Rent payable account	Dr	£1,500
Electricity account	Cr	£800
Interest receivable account	Dr	£300
Provision for doubtful debts account	Cr	£4,800

You are told the following:

- Rent is payable quarterly in advance on the last day of November, February, May and August, at the rate of £6,000 per annum.

- Electricity is paid as follows:

5 November 20X5	£1,000 (for the period to 31 October 20X5)
10 February 20X6	£1,300 (for the period to 31 January 20X6)
8 May 20X6	£1,500 (for the period to 30 April 20X6)
7 August 20X6	£1,100 (for the period to 31 July 20X6)

    At 30 September 20X6, the electricity meter shows that £900 has been consumed since the last bill was received.

- Interest was received during the year as follows:

2 October 20X5	£250 (for the six months to 30 September 20X5)
3 April 20X6	£600 (for the six months to 31 March 20X6)

    You estimate that interest of £300 is accrued at 30 September 20X6.

- At 30 September 20X6, the balance of debtors amounts to £125,000. The provision for doubtful debts is to be amended to 5% of debtors.

Required:

(a) Write up the ledger accounts for:

    (i) rent payable;

    (ii) electricity;

    (iii) interest receivable;

    (iv) allowance for doubtful debts

and bring down the balances at 30 September 20X6. **(11 marks)**

(b) State the meaning of EACH of the four balances brought down on the accounts at 30 September 20X6, AND show how they should be treated in the balance sheet at 30 September 20X6. **(4 marks)**

(Total: 15 marks)

QUESTION 3

RBD

The ledger of RBD & Co included the following ledger balances:

	1 June 20X0 £	31 May 20X1 £
Rents receivable: prepayments	463	517
Rent and rates payable: prepayments	1,246	1,509
accruals	315	382
Creditors	5,258	4,720
Provision for discounts on creditors	106	94

During the year ended 31 May 20X1 the following transactions had arisen:

	£
Rents received by cheque	4,058
Rent paid by cheque	7,491
Rates paid by cheque	2,805
Creditors paid by cheque	75,181
Discounts received from creditors	1,043
Purchases on credit	to be derived

Required:

Post and balance the appropriate accounts for the year ended 31 May 20X1, deriving the transfer entries to the profit and loss account where applicable.

(15 marks)

QUESTION 4

PDS

PDS operates a manual bookkeeping system. An examination of the accounts paid for motor expenses reveals the following:

Petrol	(paid one month in arrears) to June X7	£1,225
	June 20X7 account received and paid July X7	£165
Car insurance	(started 1 October 20X6) for year to 30 September X7	£1,200
Car licenses	(paid September 20X6) for six months to 31 March 20X7	£80
	(paid March 20X7) for year to 31 March 20X8	£140

Servicing and repairs accounts amounted to £1,500 for work carried out and invoiced in the period to 30 June 20X7. An invoice for £350 was received in August 20X7 for work carried out in June 20X7.

Required:

(a) Make the appropriate entries in the motor expenses account for the year ended 30 June 20X7.

(b) Balance off the account as at that date using an accruals account and a prepayments account.

(c) Make the opening entries in the motor expenses account as at 1 July 20X7.

(15 marks)

QUESTION 5

SBJ

SBJ's fixed asset register gives the cost and depreciation to date for every fixed asset held by the company. Prior to charging depreciation for 20X4, the total net book value of all fixed assets on the register at 31 December 20X4, was £147,500.

At the same date, the fixed asset accounts in the nominal ledger showed the following balances:

	Cost	Depreciation to date
	£	£
Motor vehicles	48,000	12,000
Plant and machinery	120,000	30,000
Office equipment	27,500	7,500

You are told that:

(i) An item of plant costing £30,000 has been sold for £23,500 during 20X4. The loss on disposal was £800. No entries have been made for this disposal in the nominal ledger, but the asset has been removed from the fixed asset register.

(ii) A motor car was purchased on 1 October 20X4, and correctly recorded in the nominal ledger. Its cost was as follows:

List price of vehicle	£24,000
Trade discount	20%
VAT added at 17.5%	
Insurance	£360
Vehicle licence (road fund) tax	£130
Painting of company name	£100 (No VAT)

The vehicle has not been entered in the fixed asset register.

(iii) Office equipment was purchased during 20X4, entered on the fixed asset register, but not in the nominal ledger. Until the omission can be investigated fully, its cost is deemed to be the difference between the balances on the fixed asset register and the nominal ledger at 31 December 20X4 (prior to charging depreciation for the year).

(iv) Depreciation for 20X4 is to be charged as follows:

- on motor vehicles, at 25% per annum straight line on an actual time basis;
- on plant and machinery, at 10% per annum straight line, with a full year's depreciation in the year of purchase;
- on office equipment, at 10% per annum reducing balance, with a full year's depreciation in the year of purchase.

Required:

(a) Calculate the correct balances at 31 December 20X4, for cost and depreciation to date on the three fixed asset accounts in the nominal ledger (prior to the charging of depreciation for 20X4). **(11 marks)**

(b) Calculate the depreciation for each class of fixed asset for 20X4. **(4 marks)**

(Total: 15 marks)

QUESTION 6

DIAMOND PLC

Diamond plc is a trading company making up its accounts regularly to 31 December each year.

At 1 January 20X5 the following balances existed in the records of Diamond plc.

	£000
Freehold land – cost	1,000
Freehold buildings – cost	500
Aggregate depreciation provided on buildings to 31.12.X4	210
Office equipment – cost	40
Aggregate depreciation provided on office equipment to 31.12.X4	24

The company's depreciation policies are as follows:

Freehold land – no depreciation.

Freehold buildings – depreciation provided at 2% per annum on cost on the straight-line basis.

Office equipment – depreciation provided at 12½% per annum on the straight-line basis.

A full year's depreciation is charged in the year of acquisition of all assets and none in the year of disposal.

During the two years to 31 December 20X6 the following transactions took place:

1 **Year ended 31 December 20X5:**

   (a)   10 June   Office equipment purchased for £16,000. This equipment was to replace some old items which were given in part exchange. Their agreed part exchange value was £4,000. They had originally cost £8,000 and their book value was £1,000. The company paid the balance of £12,000 in cash.

   (b)   8 October   An extension was made to the building at a cost of £50,000.

2 **Year ended 31 December 20X6:**

   1 March   Office equipment which had cost £8,000 and with a written-down value of £2,000 was sold for £3,000.

Required:

Write up the necessary ledger accounts to record these transactions for the *two* years ended 31 December 20X6. (Separate cost and aggregate depreciation accounts are required – you should NOT combine cost and depreciation in a single account.)

(15 marks)

QUESTION 7

A CLIENT

You are finalising the accounts of a client for the year to 30 April 20X4. During the year the client acquired a new motor vehicle. In the working papers you note the following:

- The new motor vehicle was purchased on 15 October 20X3 and was financed by a loan of £9,000 and a trade in allowance of £10,500 on a car which had been purchased for £15,000 on 17 September 20X2.

- Depreciation on motor vehicles is provided on a straight line basis at a rate of 20% per annum.

- Assets are depreciated from the beginning of the month following their acquisition. A full month's depreciation is charged in the month of disposal of an asset.

- The balances brought forward at 1 May 20X3 were:

	Cost	Accumulated depreciation
Motor vehicles	£37,200	£15,890

Required:

(a) Calculate the accumulated depreciation as at 15 October 20X3 on the car traded in.

(4 marks)

(b) Calculate the profit or loss arising on the disposal of the car traded in. **(4 marks)**

(c) Calculate the depreciation charge on Motor Vehicles for the year to 30 April 20X4.

(4 marks)

(d) Prepare the Motor Vehicles at Cost account for the year to 30 April 20X4. **(5 marks)**

Note: In part (d) you MUST use a format which clearly identifies the debit and credit entries.

(Total: 17 marks)

QUESTION 8

DEBBIE FRASER

Debbie Fraser prepares her accounts to 31 October each year. During the year to 31 October 20X3, she traded in her old car which she had purchased in November 20X0 for £12,800. She receive a trade in allowance of £6,500 and paid a cheque for £8,200 to the dealer for the new car.

Debbie's policy is to provide for depreciation on motor vehicles at a rate of 25% per annum on the reducing balance basis. She charges a full year's depreciation in the year of purchase, and no charge is made in the year of disposal.

Required:

(a)   Calculate the amount of depreciation which will be charged in the accounts for the year to 31 October 20X3 for the new car.   **(2 marks)**

(b)   Calculate the profit or loss on the disposal of the old car.   **(4 marks)**

(c)   How will the profit or loss on the disposal of the old car be dealt with in Debbie's accounts for the year to 31 October 20X3?   **(2 marks)**

(d)   Show Debbie's motor vehicles at cost account for the year to 31 October 20X3.   **(5 marks)**

(*Note:* You MUST use a format which clearly indicates whether your entries are debits or credits.)

(e)   Briefly explain the difference between the reducing balance method and the straight line method of providing for depreciation.   **(2 marks)**

(Total: 15 marks)

QUESTION 9

RAMSEY

The following figures have been extracted from the books of Ramsey as at 31 December 20X8:

Trial balance as at 31 Dec 20X8

	Dr £	Cr £
Capital		24,860
Sales		94,360
Purchases	48,910	
Fixed assets, at cost	32,750	
Provision for depreciation		11,500
Debtors	17,190	
Bank	18,100	
Creditors		11,075
Stock at 1 Jan 20X8	8,620	
Rent	4,200	
Electricity	2,150	
Drawings	9,875	
	141,795	141,795

The following additional information is provided:

(a) The stock at 31 December 20X8 is £9,180.

(b) Depreciation for the year is to be charged at 10% of the cost of the fixed assets.

(c) Rent of £300 is prepaid for 20X9.

(d) Electricity of £250 is still owing on 31 December 20X8.

Required:

Prepare an extended trial balance for Ramsey as at 31 December 20X8 showing clearly the profit for the year.

(15 marks)

QUESTION 10

JANE SIMPSON

Jane Simpson, a retail trader, has been trying to keep her own accounting records and has extracted the following list of balances as at 30 April 20X9 from her accounts prior to the preparation of the annual accounts and balance sheet by James Lang, an accountant and your employer.

	£
Fixtures and fittings	5,000
Motor vehicles	4,000
Stock in trade	12,000
Trade debtors	7,000
Balance at bank (asset)	1,700
Trade creditors	6,900
Sales	132,000
Cost of sales	79,200
Establishment and administrative expenses	11,800
Sales and distribution expenses	33,500
Drawings	9,700
Capital	30,000

In reviewing the information, James Lang makes a number of discoveries which he passes on to you.

MEMORANDUM

From: James Lang

To: You

Date:

Subject: Accounts for Jane Simpson for year ended 30 April 20X9

Can you do some initial work on the enclosed accounts? I think there are some errors. In particular I have discovered:

(i) an entry in the cash book for the purchase of fixtures and fittings on 1 February 20X9 costing £4,500 has not been posted to the ledger;

(ii) a credit sale of £4,700 in March 20X9 was included correctly in the posting to the sales account, but recorded as £4,200 in the debtor's account;

(iii) goods costing £600 withdrawn by Jane Simpson for her own use have not been recorded in the accounts. This should be treated as a reduction in the figure for purchases.

Required:

(a) Prepare Jane Simpson's uncorrected trial balance as at 30 April 20X9, including a suspense account as the balancing figure. **(5 marks)**

(b) Prepare journal entries for the errors discovered. **(6 marks)**

(c) Prepare a new trial balance showing the corrected amounts. **(4 marks)**

(Total: 15 marks)

QUESTION 11

JEFFREY

Jeffrey's trial balance at 30 September 20X4 is shown below:

	Dr £	Cr £
Capital at 1 October 20X3		30,217
Stock at 1 October 20X3	12,560	
Debtors	12,880	
Creditors and accruals		6,561
Bank	4,754	
Sales		90,560
Returns inward	375	
Purchases	72,674	
Carriage inwards	974	
Wages	4,684	
Rent	3,200	
Stationery	382	
Travel	749	
Telephone	853	
General expenses	753	
Drawings	12,500	
	127,338	127,338

The value of Jeffrey's stock at 30 September 20X4 was £11,875.

Jeffrey has discovered the following errors in the postings:

(i) An invoice for carriage inwards was posted to the returns inwards account. The invoice was for £264.

(ii) A credit sale invoice for £560 was posted as £650.

(iii) The telephone bill for the three months to 30 September 20X4, which was received after the year end, has not been included. The bill is for £297.

Required:

(a) Indicate which of the balances in the trial balance will be changed by the correction of the errors, and calculate the corrected balances. **(6 marks)**

(b) Based on the corrected trial balance, calculate:

　(i) the gross profit and the net profit for the year to 30 September 20X4; **(7 marks)**

　(ii) the capital balance at 30 September 20X4. **(2 marks)**

(Total: 15 marks)

QUESTION 12

YATTON

Yatton does not keep proper books of account. You ascertain that his bank payments and receipts during the year to 31 December 20X8 were as follows:

Bank account

	£		£
Balance 1 Jan 20X8	800	Cash withdrawn	200
Cheques for sales	2,500	Purchases	2,500
Cash banked	3,000	Expenses	800
		Drawings	1,300
		Delivery van (bought 1 Oct 20X8)	1,000
		Balance 31 Dec 20X8	500
	6,300		6,300

From a cash notebook you ascertain that:

	£
Cash in hand 1 January 20X8	70
Cash takings	5,200
Purchases paid in cash	400
Expenses paid in cash	500
Cash in hand 31 December 20X8	30
Drawings by proprietor in cash	unknown

You discover that assets and liabilities were as follows:

	1 Jan 20X8 £	31 Dec 20X8 £
Debtors	300	450
Trade creditors	800	900
Expense creditors	100	150
Stock on hand	1,400	1,700

Yatton says that he has no hope of receiving an amount of £100 due from one customer and that a provision of 10% of debtors would be prudent. Depreciation on the van is to be provided at the rate of 20% per annum.

Required:

(a) Prepare a profit and loss account for the year ended 31 December 20X8. **(10 marks)**

(b) Calculate Yatton's closing capital. **(5 marks)**

(Total: 15 marks)

QUESTION 13

TOM WEST

Tom West has been trading part time for four years as a supplier of computer software. In the past he has not completed full accounts for his business, but has simply made a return of income and expenses to the tax authorities. He wishes to prepare full accounts in future years and has provided the following information:

(i) He began trading on I July 20X5 and prepares his income and expenses figures for the year to 30 June. When he began trading he had bought computer equipment at a cost of £4,500. He estimates that computer equipment has a useful life of five years.

(ii) His income, expenses (excluding depreciation) and drawings for the three years to 30 June 20X8 were:

	Income £	Expenses £	Drawings £
Year to 30 June 20X6	1,200	400	300
Year to 30 June 20X7	3,500	1,200	1,800
Year to 30 June 20X8	5,700	2,900	2,700

Note: All income received was paid into the bank account, and all expenses and drawings were paid by cheque.

(iii) He has no costs in respect of goods for resale as the nature of his business is to create computer software to clients' specifications.

(iv) At 30 June 20X8 he still had to collect £900 from customers. At 30 June 20X9 he still had to collect £2,700.

(v) In the year to 30 June 20X9 he had paid £14,000 into his bank account. This had been received from clients for work completed with the exception of £3,000 which was a gift from a relative.

(vi) During the year to 30 June 20X9 he had paid the following amounts by cheque:

	£
Stationery	250
Motor expenses	790
Electricity	560
Repairs	425
Travel	615
Office Furniture	1,400
Drawings	4,600
	8,640

(vii) Depreciation is provided on a straight line basis at the following rates:

Computer equipment   20% per annum
Office furniture   10% per annum

A full year's depreciation is provided in the year of acquisition of an asset.

Required:

(a) Calculate Tom West's capital at 30 June 20X8. **(5 marks)**

(b) Calculate Tom West's profit for the year to 30 June 20X9. **(6 marks)**

(c) Calculate Tom West's capital at 30 June 20X9. **(4 marks)**

(Total: 15 marks)

QUESTION 14

SIMON MEREDITH

Simon Meredith has been trading for some years. His accounting records have been destroyed, but he has been able to provide you with some information for the year ended 30 November 20X1.

- During the year he paid £298,000 into his business bank account.
- Apart from £25,000 introduced as additional capital, this represented payments received from his customers.
- All receipts were paid immediately into the bank account.
- At 30 November 20X1 he has owed £31,500 by his customers and he owed £22,700 to his suppliers.
- His stock at 30 November 20X1 had cost £17,500.
- During the year he issued cheques totally £295,300.
- Apart from payments to suppliers, the cheques issued were as follows:

    – various business expenses   £32,000
    – purchase of a new van   £11,000
    – drawings   £15,000

On 30 November 20X0:

- Simon was owed £29,720 by his customers.
- He owed £23,900 to his suppliers.
- His stock was valued at £16,800.

Required:

(a) Calculate the value of Simon's sales for the year to 30 November 20X1. **(6 marks)**

(b) Calculate Simon's gross profit for the year to 30 November 20X1. **(9 marks)**

(Total: 15 marks)

QUESTION 15

J PATEL

The assets and liabilities as at the close of business on 31 October 20X8 of J Patel, retailer, are summarised as follows:

	£	£
Motor vehicles		
At cost	9,000	
Provision for depreciation	1,800	
		7,200
Fixtures and fittings		
At cost	10,000	
Provision for depreciation	6,000	
		4,000
Stock		16,100
Trade debtors		19,630
Cash		160
		47,090
Capital – J Patel		30,910
Bank overdraft		6,740
Trade creditors		9,440
		47,090

All receipts from credit customers are paid intact into the business bank account whilst cash sales receipts are banked after deduction of cash drawings and providing for the shop till cash float. The cash float was increased from £160 to £200 in September 20X9.

The following is a summary of the transactions in the business bank account for the year ended 31 October 20X9:

Bank account

Receipts	£	Payments	£
Credit sales	181,370	Drawings	8,500
Cash sales	61,190	Motor van (bought 1 May 20X9)	11,200
Proceeds of sale of land owned owned privately by J Patel	16,000	Purchases	163,100
		Establishment and administrative expenses	33,300
		Sales and distribution expenses	29,100

Additional information for the year ended 31 October 20X9:

(a) Credit sales amount to £173,770.

(b) Bad debts of £530 have been written off during the year.

(c) Purchases in the year amounted to £166,360.

(d) Depreciation is to be provided at the following annual rates on cost:

> Motor vehicles   20%
> Fixtures and fittings   10%

(e) Stock at 31 October 20X9 has been valued at £23,700.

Required:

Prepare a balance sheet as at 31 October 20X9 for J Patel.

(15 marks)

QUESTION 16

R THOMAS

R Thomas is a successful sole trader, but is not particularly good at maintaining financial records. He asks you to prepare his final accounts for the year to 31 May 20X9. You establish that at 1 June 20X8 he had the following balances:

	£000
Vehicles at cost	100
Equipment at cost	200
Provisions for depreciation	
Vehicles	50
Equipment	80
Trade creditors	170
Trade debtors	225
Prepayments	
Rent	12
Insurance	15
Accruals	
Telephone	4
Electricity	6
Bank	28
Stock	150
Capital	420

In addition R Thomas is also able to provide the following information for the financial year to 31 May 20X9.

(i) Receipts from customers were £1,200,000 and there are trade debtors at 31 May 20X9 of £230,000.

(ii) Irrecoverable debts of £35,000 were written off during the year and discounts to customers amounted to £30,000.

(iii) Personal drawings amounted to £100,000.

(iv) Payments to suppliers were £650,000, and £155,000 was owing to suppliers as at 31 May 20X9.

(v) Stock at 31 May 20X9 was £190,000.

(vi) Rent of £10,000 and telephone bills of £1,000 were paid in advance at 31 May 20X9.

(vii) A £15,000 electricity bill was still to be paid at 31 May 20X9.

(viii) Other payments made during the year were as follows:

	£000
Insurance	25
Rent	40
Rates	5
Electricity	30
Telephone	14
Motor vehicle expenses	20
Wages	120
	254

(ix) Depreciation on vehicles is provided annually at a rate of 25% on their original cost. Depreciation on equipment is based on 20% of its written down value.

Required:

Prepare the following statements for R Thomas:

(a) the trading and profit and loss account for the year ended 31 May 20X9 **(26 marks)**

(b) the balance sheet as at 31 May 20X9. **(14 marks)**

Show any necessary supporting workings.

(Total: 40 marks)

QUESTION 17

AMBER, BERYL AND CORAL

Amber and Beryl are in partnership sharing profits in the ratio 60:40 after charging annual salaries of £20,000 each. they regularly make up their accounts to 31 December each year.

On 1 July 20X6 they admitted Coral as a partner and agreed profit shares from that date of 40% Amber, 40% Beryl and 20% Coral. The salaries credited to Amber and Beryl ceased from 1 July 20X6.

The partnership trial balance at 31 December 20X6 was as follows:

	£	£
Capital accounts as at 1.1.X6:		
Amber		280,000
Beryl		210,000
Capital account Coral (see note (iv) below)		140,000
Current accounts as at 1.1.X6		
Amber		7,000
Beryl		6,000
Drawings accounts		
Amber	28,000	
Beryl	24,000	
Coral	15,000	
Loan account Amber		50,000
Sales		2,000,000
Purchases	1,400,000	
Stock 1.1.X6	180,000	
Wages and salaries of staff	228,000	
Sundry expenses	120,000	
Allowance for doubtful debts at 1.1.X6		20,000
Freehold land at cost (see note (v) below)	200,000	
Buildings:		
Cost	250,000	
Aggregate depreciation 1.1.X6		30,000
Plant, equipment and vehicles:		
Cost	240,000	
Aggregate depreciation 1.1.X6		50,000
Trade debtors and creditors	420,000	350,000
Cash at bank	38,000	
	3,143,000	3,143,000

In preparing the partnership accounts the following further information is to be taken into account:

(i) Closing stock at 31 December 20X6 was £200,000.

(ii) Debts totalling £16,000 are to be written off and the allowance for doubtful debts increased by £10,000.

(iii) Staff bonuses totalling £12,000 were unpaid at 31 December 20X6.

(iv) The balance of £140,000 on Coral's capital account consists of £100,000 introduced as capital and a further sum of £40,000 paid for a 20% share of the goodwill of the partnership. The appropriate adjustments to deal with the goodwill payment are to be made in the capital accounts of the partners concerned, and no goodwill account is to remain in the records.

(v) It was agreed that the freehold land should be revalued upwards on 30 June prior to the admission of Coral from £200,000 to £280,000. The revised value is to appear in the balance sheet at 31 December 20X6.

(vi) Amber's loan carries interest at 10% per annum and was advanced to the partnership some years ago.

(vii) Provide depreciation on the straight-line basis on cost as follows:

Buildings	2%
Plant, equipment and vehicles	10%

(viii) Profits accrued evenly during the year.

Required:

(a) Prepare a trading account, profit and loss account and appropriation account for the year ended 31 December 20X6 and a balance sheet as at that date. **(17 marks)**

(b) Prepare the partners' capital accounts and current accounts for the year in columnar form.
(7 marks)

(Total: 24 marks)

QUESTION 18

SMITH, JONES AND MATTHEWS

Smith, Jones and Matthews are in partnership and their trial balance for the year ended 30 September 20X8 was as follows:

	Dr £	Cr £
Motor vans at cost	43,750	
Office equipment at cost	29,400	
Provisions for depreciation at 1 October 20X7:		
Motor vans		14,700
Office equipment		9,450
Sales		736,750
Carriage inwards	5,250	
Stock at 1 October 20X7	149,975	
Discounts allowed	385	
Returns inwards	23,800	
Irrecoverable debts	4,319	
Allowance for doubtful debts		2,800
General expenses	3,308	
Rent and rates	8,978	
Postages	8,575	
Motor expenses	13,790	
Salaries and wages	64,036	
Purchases	480,165	
Drawings:		
Smith	44,135	
Jones	29,460	
Matthews	21,756	
Current accounts at 1 October 20X7:		
Smith		7,260
Jones		4,865
Matthews	536	
Capital accounts		
Smith		105,000
Jones		56,000
Matthews		42,000
Creditors		85,246
Debtors	130,123	
Cash at bank	2,330	
	1,064,071	1,064,071

The following additional information is also available:

(i) Stock at 30 September 20X8 was £178,710.

(ii) Rates of £420 were paid in advance at 30 September 20X8.

(iii) The allowance for doubtful debts is to be increased to £3,045 and any adjustment charged to irrecoverable debts.

(iv) The provision for depreciation for year ended 30 September 20X8 is to be: motor vans £8,750 and office equipment £5,880.

(v) Included in drawings are salaries as follows: Smith £4,200, Jones £2,450 and Matthews £3,500.

(vi) Interest on drawings is: Smith £595, Jones £385 and Matthews £420.

(vii) Interest on each partner's capital is to be allowed for at 10% per annum.

(viii) Smith, Jones and Matthews have agreed that profits and losses should be shared in the ratio 6:4:2 respectively.

Required:

You are required to prepare the following statements for the partnership for the year ended 30 September 20X8:

(a) the trading and profit and loss account (including an appropriation account) **(20 marks)**

(b) the partners' current accounts **(6 marks)**

(c) the balance sheet as at 30 September 20X8. **(14 marks)**

Supporting workings are required.

(Total: 40 marks)

QUESTION 19

CAIN AND ABEL

Cain and Abel have been in partnership for several years and share profits and losses in the ratio 3:2. The following is the trial balance from the partnership books as at 31 October 20X0:

		Dr £	Cr £
Allowance for doubtful debts			6,000
Sales			1,483,400
Accumulated depreciation	– Vans		66,600
	– Fittings		12,800
Office expenses		72,000	
Purchases		1,143,400	
Bank			7,650
Vans at cost		90,000	
Fittings at cost		28,000	
Debtors		137,200	
Creditors			47,200
Stock at 1 November 20W9		195,300	
Insurance		8,650	
Motor vehicle expenses		44,500	
Motor car, at cost (purchased 1 November 20W9)		18,000	
Discounts allowed		28,800	
Wages and salaries		82,800	
Capital accounts at 1 November 20W9	– Cain		154,000
	– Abel		138,000
Drawings	– Cain	40,000	
	– Abel	27,000	
		1,915,650	1,915,650

The following additional information as at 31 October 20X0 is available:

(1) Bank charges of £655 have not been entered into the accounts.

(2) Depreciation is to be provided for, using the reducing balance method at 10% on fittings and 20% on vans and the motor car. Abel is to accept personally £5,000 of the motor vehicle expenses and half of the depreciation charge on the motor car.

(3) Stock was valued at £296,700.

(4) The partners are entitled to 10% a year on capital.

(5) Insurance of £850 has been paid in advance.

(6) There are outstanding wages of £3,475.

(7) The annual payment for rent of £9,000 is still outstanding.

(8) £2,200 of irrecoverable debts are to be written off.

(9) The allowance for doubtful debts is to be adjusted to 5% of the remaining debtors and the adjustment charged to irrecoverable debts.

(10) Interest on drawings for the year is: Cain £2,400; Abel £1,420.

(11) There were no current account balances at 1 November 20W9.

Required:

(a) Prepare the following statements for the partnership:

    (i) the trading and profit and loss account (including an appropriation account) for the year ended 31 October 20X0 **(18 marks)**

    (ii) the partners' current accounts for the year ended 31 October 20X0 **(6 marks)**

    (iii) the balance sheet as at 31 October 20X0. **(12 marks)**

(b) Briefly outline the advantages and disadvantages of operating as a partnership rather than as a sole trader. **(4 marks)**

(Total: 40 marks)

QUESTION 20

JACK AND JILL

Until 31 January 20X3 Jack and Jill were business partners, sharing profits in the ratio 2:1 respectively, after allowing for interest on capital of 6%. On 1 February 20X3 Jean was admitted to the partnership. She is to receive a one-sixth share of the profits for introducing £40,000 capital and £30,000 as her share of goodwill.

The trial balance extracted from the partnership books on 31 May 20X3, the end of the financial year, is as follows:

Jack, Jill and Jean – Trial balance as at 31 May 20X3

		Dr £000	Cr £000
Fittings at cost		210	
Vehicles at cost		180	
Stock as at 1 June 20X2		190	
Purchases		725	
Sales			979
Rent and insurance		33	
Sales commission		18	
Debtors		140	
Creditors			154
Cash and bank		33	
Advertising and other expenses		52	
Discounts allowed		25	
Bad debts		7	
Fittings depreciation to 31 May 20X2			60
Vehicle depreciation to 31 May 20X2			40
Drawings:	Jack	25	
	Jill	10	
	Jean	2	
Capital:	Jack		250
	Jill		100
Current accounts:	Jack		12
	Jill	15	
Suspense account			70
		1,665	1,665

Additional notes

(i) Stock on 31 May 20X3 was £214,000.

(ii) There is outstanding sales commission of £2,000 for the year.

(iii) Insurance of £1,000 has been paid in advance.

(iv) The partnership depreciates fittings and vehicles at 10% and 20% respectively using the reducing balance method.

(v) Goodwill is to be adjusted for, but is not to be maintained in the books of account.

(vi) Assume that income and expenditure has accrued evenly throughout the year.

(vii) The suspense account represents the investment made by Jean.

Required:

(a) Calculate the new profit-sharing ratio as from 1 February 20X3. **(3 marks)**

(b) Calculate the new balances on the partners' capital accounts as at 1 February 20X3. **(5 marks)**

(c) Prepare the trading, profit and loss and appropriation accounts for the year ended 31 May 20X3. **(16 marks)**

(d) Prepare the partners' current accounts for the year ended 31 May 20X3. **(7 marks)**

(e) Prepare the balance sheet as at 31 May 20X3. **(9 marks)**

(Calculations and workings should be rounded to the nearest £000.)

(Total: 40 marks)

QUESTION 21

LINCOLN PLC

You are presented with the following trial balances of Lincoln plc as at 31 December 20X9.

	£000	£000
Share capital, 50p ordinary shares		1,000
Share premium		500
15% Debentures		800
Profit and loss balance 1 January		200
Purchases and sales	2,400	5,000
Purchase returns and sales returns	100	150
Sales and purchase ledger control balances	1,000	400
Property – cost	800	
– depreciation to 1.1.X9		200
Land – at valuation on 1.1.X1	900	
Machinery – cost	1,600	
– depreciation to 1.1.X9		500
Discounts for prompt payment	20	10
Operating expenses	1,300	
Dividends paid	100	
Debenture interest paid to 1.7.X9	60	
Bank		30
Suspense account	210	
Stock at 1.1.X9	300	
	8,790	8,790

The bookkeeper has not recorded certain items, and seems to have only partially recorded others. Details are given below.

(i) Half of the debentures had been redeemed on 1 July 20X9 at a cost of £380,000. Only one entry, in the bank account, had been made.

(ii) During the year 20X9, 200,000 more ordinary shares, identical to those already in issue, had been issued at 110 pence per share. Again only one entry, in the bank account, had been made.

(iii) The managing director has taken £10,000 of the purchases for his own use and no entries have been made for this.

(iv) The land is to be revalued, as at 31 December 20X9, at £1,500,000.

(v) Depreciation of 2% pa on cost needs to be provided on the property.

(vi) One tenth of the cost of machinery figure represents items which were fully depreciated down to their estimated scrap value of £10,000 prior to 1 January 20X9. There have been no purchases or disposals of machinery during 20X9. Depreciation of 10% pa on the reducing balance basis needs to be provided on the machinery, as appropriate.

(vii) An amount of £50,000 had been paid during the year 20X9 to a customer because of personal injury he had suffered as a result of a fault in the goods delivered to him. Only one entry, in the cash book, had been made.

(viii) Closing stock at 31 December 20X2 is £400,000. Half of this figure represents purchases still included in the purchase ledger control account balance at 31 December 20X2.

(ix) Any balance on the suspense account should be shown in the profit and loss account as a separate item.

Required:

Prepare the profit and loss account and balance sheet of Lincoln plc, in good order, as at 31 December 20X9. Your layout and use of headings and sub-totals should be designed to give the maximum of helpful information to the reader. All necessary workings should be clearly shown.

(25 marks)

QUESTION 22

BOWDERRY CO LTD

The Chief Accountant has presented you with the following balances for Bowderry Co Ltd for the year ended 31 May 20X8.

	£
Creditors	39,800
Sales	500,000
Land at cost	206,400
Buildings at cost	240,000
Furniture and fittings at cost	140,000
Bank overdraft	49,100
Provisions for depreciation at 1 June 20X7:	
Buildings	36,000
Furniture and fittings	60,000
Discounts received	12,400
Profit and loss account at 1 June 20X7	12,000
Allowance for doubtful debts	5,196
Cash in hand	1,424
Stock at 1 June 20X7	91,788
Interim dividend on preference shares	3,900
Rates	15,000
Wages and salaries	50,000
Insurance	12,500
Returns inward	2,732
General expenses	3,120
Debtors	96,140
Purchases	264,636
Debenture interest	4,800
Irrecoverable debts	4,056
10% Debentures	96,000
6% £1 Preference shares	130,000
£1 Ordinary shares	130,000
Fixed asset replacement reserve	60,000
Share premium account	6,000

You discover from various sources the following information:

(i) Stock at 31 May 20X8 was £95,500.

(ii) Insurance has been paid £700 in advance at 31 May 20X8.

(iii) There were wages owing to staff of £1,900 at 31 May 20X8.

(iv) Depreciation for the year ended 31 May 20X8 is to be provided at 10% of the cost of buildings and at 20% of the written down value of furniture and fittings.

(v) Debenture interest outstanding at 31 May 20X8 is £4,800.

(vi) Allowance for doubtful debts is to be reduced to 5% of debtors and any adjustments charged to irrecoverable debts.

(vii) The directors propose to pay the final preference dividend and to pay a final dividend of 12% on ordinary shares. These proposals were announced before the year end.

(viii) The directors propose a transfer of £30,000 to the fixed asset replacement reserve.

(ix) The corporation tax charge for the year is £40,000 and should be provided for.

Required:

Prepare the following statements, for internal use, for the year ending 31 May 20X8:

(a) the profit and loss account **(26 marks)**

(b) the balance sheet. **(14 marks)**

Supporting workings are required for which there are marks available.

(Total: 40 marks)

QUESTION 23

ARNFIELD LTD

The following trial balance has been prepared for Arnfield Ltd for the year ended 31 October 20X9:

	Dr £000	Cr £000
Buildings at cost	2,000	
Motor vehicles at cost	70	
Land at cost	600	
Furniture and equipment at cost	1,000	
Fixed assets replacement reserve		100
Share premium account		40
Cash in hand	140	
Stock at 1 November 20X8	700	
Rates	100	
Advertising	30	
Insurance	70	
Wages and salaries	750	
Heating and lighting	80	
Discounts received		130
Profit and loss account at 1 November 20X8		100
Allowance for doubtful debts		40
Returns inward	30	
General expenses	20	
Telephone	40	
Sales		7,900
Creditors		320
Bank		300
Debtors	1,960	
Purchases	3,500	
Debenture interest	50	
Irrecoverable debts	600	
Provisions for depreciation at 1 November 20X8		
Furniture and equipment		350
Buildings		400
Motor vehicles		20
10% Debentures		500
6% £1 Preference shares		300
£1 Ordinary shares		1,240
	11,740	11,740

You have also been provided with the following notes:

(1) Stock at 31 October 20X9 was valued at £900,000.

(2) The advertising expenditure included £10,000 which relates to a newspaper advertising campaign to be run during November and December 20X9.

(3) There are wages and salaries outstanding of £70,000 for the year ended 31 October 20X9.

(4) The allowance for doubtful debts is to be increased to £50,000 and any adjustments charged to irrecoverable debts.

Depreciation is to be provided for as follows:

Motor vehicles at 20% of written down value

(5) Furniture and equipment at 20% of written down value.

(6) Buildings are depreciated at 10% of cost. At 31 October 20X9 the buildings were professionally valued at £2,300,000 and the directors wish this valuation to be incorporated into the accounts.

(7) An additional £150,000 is to be transferred to the fixed assets replacement reserve.

(8) Corporation tax of £700,000 is to be provided for the year.

Required:

Prepare the following statements, for internal use:

(a) the profit and loss account for the year ended 31 October 20X9 **(25 marks)**

(b) the balance sheet as at 31 October 20X9. **(15 marks)**

You are advised to show workings where appropriate.

(Total: 40 marks)

QUESTION 24

MUGGERIDGE LTD

The trial balance of Muggeridge Ltd at 31 December 20X9 was as follows:

	Dr £000	Cr £000
7% Preference shares of 50p		500
Ordinary shares of £1		250
Share premium account		180
Profit and loss account, at 1 January 20X9		40
Stock, 1 January 20X9	450	
Land at cost	300	
Buildings at cost	900	
Buildings, accumulated depreciation, 1 January 20X9		135
Plant at cost	1,020	
Plant, accumulated depreciation, 1 January 20X9		370
Trade creditors		900
Debtors	600	
Allowance for doubtful debts, at 1 January 20X9		25
Purchases	1,900	
Discounts received		70
Discounts allowed	60	
Carriage in	90	
Wages	215	
Sales		3,000
Directors' remuneration	50	
Heating and lighting	230	
Other expenses	50	
Fixed asset replacement reserve		30
Bank balance	135	
10% Debentures		500
	6,000	6,000

Additional information as at 31 December 20X9

(i)   Depreciation on buildings is provided at 5% per annum on cost.

(ii) Plant is depreciated at 20% per annum using the reducing balance method.

(iii) Closing stock is valued at £500,000.

(iv) The allowance for doubtful debts is to be made equal to 5% of debtors.

(v)   There is a wages accrual of £30,000.

(vi) Debenture interest has not been paid during the year.

(vii) On 1 January 20X9 the company purchased and absorbed another business as a going concern. Muggeridge Ltd acquired the business's sole asset of stock for £40,000 and, in addition, paid £100,000 for goodwill. The consideration of £140,000 was paid for by the issue of 100,000 ordinary shares. This transaction has not yet been recorded in the books of Muggeridge Ltd. The purchased goodwill has an estimated economic life of 10 years from 1 January 20X9.

(viii) During December a bonus (or scrip) issue of two for five was made to ordinary shareholders. This has not been entered into the books. The share premium account is to be used for this purpose.

(ix) The Directors wish to provide for a transfer of £20,000 to the fixed asset replacement reserve.

(x) Provision for corporation tax of £55,000 for the year is to be made.

Required:

(a) Prepare the following statements for Muggeridge Ltd for internal use:

  (i)   the profit and loss account for the year ended 31 December 20X9   **(18 marks)**

  (ii) the balance sheet as at 31 December 20X9.   **(16 marks)**

(b) Briefly explain the nature and purpose of a bonus (or scrip) issue.   **(3 marks)**

(Total: 37 marks)

QUESTION 25

RP ATTON LTD

RP Atton Ltd has provided you with the following trial balance as at 31 May 20X3.

	Dr £000	Cr £000
Cash in hand	10	
Stock at 1 June 20X2	650	
General expenses	25	
Insurance	45	
Advertising	35	
Wages and salaries	800	
Heating and lighting	70	
Fixed assets replacement reserve		50
Share premium account		120
Discounts received		100
Land at cost	550	
Buildings at cost	2,500	
Motor vehicles at cost	160	
Furniture and equipment at cost	1,500	
Profit and loss account at 1 June 20X2		142
Allowance for doubtful debts		35
Telephone	25	
Business rates	75	
Sales		8,500
Returns inward	85	
Trade creditors		310
Bank		123
Debtors	1,400	
Purchases	3,300	
Debenture interest	40	
Bad debts	500	
8% Debentures		500
9% £1 Preference shares		200
£1 Ordinary shares		1,000
Provisions for depreciation at 1 June 20X2		
Buildings		330
Motor vehicles		60
Furniture and equipment		300
	11,770	11,770

You have also been provided with the following information:

(1) Stock at 31 May 20X3 was valued at £500,000.

(2) The insurance expenditure includes £11,000 which relates to June 20X3 to August 20X3.

(3) There are wages and salaries outstanding of £65,000 for the year ended 31 May 20X3.

(4) The allowance for doubtful debts is to be increased to 5% of debtors.

(5) Buildings are depreciated at 5% of cost. At 31 May 20X3 the buildings were professionally valued at £2,700,000 and the directors wish this valuation to be incorporated into the accounts.

(6) Depreciation is to be provided for as follows.

(i) Motor vehicles at 20% of written down value.

(ii) Furniture and equipment at 20% of cost.

(7) During May 20X3 a bonus (or scrip) issue of one for ten was made to ordinary shareholders. This has not been entered into the books. The share premium account is to be used for this purpose.

(8) An additional £250,000 is to be transferred to the fixed asset replacement reserve.

(9) Corporation tax of £500,000 is to be provided for the year.

Required:

Prepare the following statements, for internal use:

(a) the trading and profit and loss account for the year ended 31 May 20X3 **(24 marks)**

(b) the balance sheet as at 31 May 20X3. **(16 marks)**

(Total: 40 marks)

QUESTION 26

POLLARD LTD

The following is the trial balance of Pollard Ltd as at 31 October 20X1:

	Dr £000	Cr £000
Stock, at 31 October 20X0	600	
Land at cost	400	
Trade creditors		450
Debtors	900	
Buildings at cost	800	
Buildings, accumulated depreciation, at 31 October 20X0		120
Plant at cost	1,400	
Plant, accumulated depreciation, at 31 October 20X0		200
7% Preference shares of £1		300
Ordinary shares of £1		700
Share premium account		200
Profit and loss account, at 31 October 20X0		80
Allowance for doubtful debts, at 31 October 20X0		50
Wages	325	
Sales		4,370
Directors' fees	100	
Heating and lighting	85	
Insurance	45	
Other expenses	30	
8% Debentures		800
Purchases	2,600	
Discounts received		60
Discounts allowed	50	
Carriage in	170	
Fixed asset replacement reserve		100
Bank balance		75
	7,505	7,505

Additional information for the year ended 31 October 20X1

(1) Closing stock is valued at £450,000.

(2) There are wages outstanding of £50,000.

(3) The allowance for doubtful debts is to be made equal to 15% of outstanding debts.

(4) Debenture interest is to be accrued for the year.

(5) Insurance of £10,000 has been prepaid.

(6) Depreciation on buildings is provided at 5% per annum using the straight line method.

(7) Plant is depreciated at 20% per annum using the reducing balance method.

(8) Provision for corporation tax of £40,000 for the year is to be made.

(9) During October a bonus (or scrip) issue of one in five was made to ordinary shareholders. This has not been entered into the books. The share premium account is to be used for this purpose.

(10) A provision is to be made for the audit fee of £55,000.

Required:

(a) Prepare the following statements for Pollard Ltd for internal use:

    (i) the trading and profit and loss account for the year ended 31 October 20X1

    (17 marks)

    (ii) the balance sheet as at 31 October 20X1. **(16 marks)**

(b) Referring to items (2), (3) and (6) in the additional information above, state the main accounting concept which is being applied in each of these adjustments. **(3 marks)**

(c) Explain what is meant by 'relevance' and 'reliability' in the context of providing useful financial information. **(4 marks)**

(Total: 40 marks)

QUESTION 27

LEWIS LTD AND GORDON LTD

You have been provided with the following information for Lewis Ltd and Gordon Ltd which are retail companies selling similar products in a similar market.

Ratio	Lewis Ltd	Gordon Ltd
Gross profit percentage	18%	30%
Net profit percentage	10%	10%
Return on capital employed (ROCE)	16%	19%
Stock turnover	21 days	40 days
Average settlement period for debtors	23 days	67 days
Average settlement period for creditors	39 days	44 days

Required:

(a) State how each ratio is calculated. **(3 marks)**

(b) Comment on the performance of the two companies as indicated by the ratios. **(8 marks)**

(c) Briefly explain what further information about the companies would be helpful in assessing their performance. **(4 marks)**

(Total: 15 marks)

QUESTION 28

G PADGETT

You are provided with the following accounting ratios for G Padgett for the year ended 31 October 20X1:

- Current ratio   1.5 times
- Acid test ratio   1.25 times
- Net assets to turnover   2.5 times
- Stock turnover   6 times
- Debtors turnover   5 times.

In addition, the following information is also available:

(1) G Padgett started in business on 1 November 20X0.

(2) Working capital at 31 October 20X1 was £15,000.

(3) Drawings during the year were £6,000.

(4) Depreciation of fixed assets during the year was £4,000 and is based on 20% of their cost.

(5) General expenses, excluding depreciation, were 26% of sales.

Required:

Prepare G Padgett's trading and profit and loss account for the year ended 31 October 20X1 and his balance sheet as at 31 October 20X1 insofar as the above information permits.

(15 marks)

QUESTION 29

BOND LTD AND FRASER LTD

Bond Ltd and Fraser Ltd are companies operating in a similar market. Your manager has asked you to help her review the performance of both companies using their financial statements which are summarised below:

Profit and loss accounts for the year ended 31 May 20X3

	Bond Ltd £000	Fraser Ltd £000
Sales	23,800	24,000
Cost of sales	17,850	16,800
Gross profit	5,950	7,200
Expenses	2,500	4,800
Profit before tax	3,450	2,400
Tax on profit	900	600
Profit for the year	2,550	1,800

Balance sheets as at 31 May 20X3

	Bond Ltd £000	Bond Ltd £000	Fraser Ltd £000	Fraser Ltd £000
Fixed assets		15,000		24,000
Current assets				
Stock	500		1,200	
Trade debtors	2,000		600	
Bank	100		–	
	2,600		1,800	
Current liabilities				
Creditors	775		150	
Overdraft	–		55	
Tax	900		600	
	1,675		805	
Net current assets		925		995
		15,925		24,995
Debentures		300		1,000
		15,625		23,995
Capital and reserves				
£1 ordinary shares		12,000		20,000
Reserves		3,625		3,995
		15,625		23,995

Required:

(a) Calculate four profitability ratios and two liquidity ratios for Bond Ltd and Fraser Ltd. Show all workings. **(12 marks)**

(b) Prepare some brief notes that comment on the performance of the two companies as indicated by the ratios you have calculated in part (a). **(8 marks)**

(Total: 20 marks)

Key Technique Answers

ANSWER 1

GAS, ELECTRICITY AND RENT

(a)

Gas account

		£			£
20X5			*20X5*		
Sept 15	Purchases day book	1,200	July 1	Balance b/d	650
Dec 14	Purchases day book	1,750			
20X6			*20X6*		
Mar 18	Purchases day book	1,695	June 30	Profit and loss	6,035
June 14	Purchases day book	1,560			
June 30	Balance c/d	480			
		6,685			6,685
			July 1	Balance b/d	480

(b) The bill for £126 (excluding VAT as, assuming the trader is a VAT registered trader, the VAT is recoverable) paid in March 20X8 represents electricity consumed over the three months to 28 February 20X8. The part of this relating to December 20X7 would normally be arrived at by time apportionment, i.e. one-third of £126 = £42. If this is added onto the figure of £396, this gives the cost of electricity consumed as £438.

(c)

Rent receivable

		£			£
20X4			*20X4*		
30 Sept	P&L a/c	3,500	30 June	Cash at bank	2,000
			30 Sept	Bal c/d	1,500
		3,500			3,500
1 Oct	Bal b/d	1,500			

The income to the profit and loss account is increased by crediting the rental income account with the £1,500 due but not yet received. The £1,500 is also carried down as a debit balance, a debtor for rental due which would be shown under current assets in the balance sheet.

ANSWER 2

XY

(a) (i)

Rent payable account

			£				£
01/10/X5	Balance b/f		1,500	30/09/X6	P&L a/c		6,000
30/11/X5	Bank		1,500	30/09/X6	Balance c/f		1,500
29/02/X6	Bank		1,500				
31/05/X6	Bank		1,500				
31/08/X6	Bank		1,500				
			7,500				7,500
1/10/X6	Balance b/f		1,500				

(ii)

Electricity account

			£				£
05/11/X5	Bank		1,000	01/10/X5	Balance b/f		800
10/02/X6	Bank		1,300	30/09/X6	P&L a/c		5,000
08/05/X6	Bank		1,500				
07/08/X6	Bank		1,100				
30/09/X6	Accrual c/f		900				
			5,800				5,800
				01/10/X6	Balance b/f		900

(iii)

Interest receivable account

			£				£
01/10/X5	Balance b/f		300	02/10/X5	Bank		250
30/09/X6	P&L a/c		850	03/04/X6	Bank		600
				30/09/X6	Accrual c/f		300
			1,150				1,150
01/10/X6	Balance b/f		300				

(iv)

Allowance for doubtful debts account

			£				£
30/09/X6	Balance c/f		6,250	01/10/X5	Balance b/f		4,800
				30/09/X6	P&L a/c		1,450
			6,250				6,250
				01/10/X6	Balance b/f		6,250

(b) The balance on the rent payable account is a prepayment. Prepayments appear under the heading 'current assets' in the balance sheet.

The balance on the electricity account is an accrual. Accruals appear under the heading 'current liabilities' in the balance sheet.

The balance on the interest receivable account is accrued income. Accrued income appears under the heading 'current assets' in the balance sheet.

The balance on the allowance for doubtful debts account is XY's best estimate of the general level of the present debtors which will not be recovered. The estimate will be based on past experience of the recoverability of XY's debts. This allowance will be deducted from the total debtors figure under the heading 'current assets' in the balance sheet.

ANSWER 3

RBD

Rents receivable

20X0		£	20X0		£
			1 June	Bal b/f	463
20X1			20X1		
31 May	Profit and loss	4,004	31 May	Bank	4,058
31 May	Bal c/f	517			
		4,521			4,521

Rent and rates payable

20X0		£	20X0		£
1 June	Bal b/f	1,246	1 June	Bal b/f	315
20X1			20X1		
31 May	Bank – rent	7,491			
31 May	Bank – rates	2,805	31 May	Profit and loss	10,100
31 May	Bal c/f	382	31 May	Bal c/f	1,509
		11,924			11,924

Creditors

20X0		£	20X0		£
			1 June	Bal b/f	5,258
20X1			20X1		
31 May	Bank	75,181	31 May	Profit and loss	
31 May	Discounts received	1,043		Purchases	75,686
31 May	Bal c/f	4,720			
		80,944			80,944

Provision for discounts on creditors

20X0		£	20X0		£
1 June	Bal b/f	106			
20X1			20X1		
			31 May	Profit and loss	12
			31 May	Bal c/f	94
		106			106

Tutorial note:

In this example the discounts received during the year of £1,043 have been debited to the creditors account and credited to discounts received, the only entry in the provision for discounts account being the decrease in provision required of £12 being debited to the profit and loss account.

An alternative treatment would be to credit the provision for discounts received account with £1,043 giving a net transfer to the profit and loss account from that account of £1,031.

ANSWER 4

PDS

Motor expenses account

		£			£
1 Jul	Cash – creditors	1,225	30 June	Prepaid insurance	300
30 June	Cash – insurance	1,200	30 June	Prepaid licenses	105
	Cash – licenses	220	30 June	Profit and loss a/c	4,255
	Cash – service, repairs	1,500			
30 June	Accrued petrol	165			
30 June	Accrued service, repairs	350			
		4,660			4,660
1 Jul	Prepayments a/c	405	1 Jul	Accruals a/c	515

Prepayments

		£			£
30 June	Motor expenses	300			
30 June	Motor expenses	105	30 June	Balance c/d	405
		405			405
1 Jul	Balance b/d	405	1 Jul	Motor expenses	405

Accruals

		£			£
30 June	Balance c/d	515	30 June	Motor expenses	165
			30 June	Motor expenses	350
		515			515
1 Jul	Motor expenses	515		Balance b/d	515

ANSWER 5

SBJ

(a) **Motor vehicles**

	£
List price	24,000
Less: 20%	(14,800)
	19,200
Add: VAT 17.5%	3,360
	22,560
Add: Cost of painting name	100
Amount to add to fixed asset register	22,660

The insurance and road fund licence are revenue costs.

Plant and machinery

	Cost £	Accumulated depreciation £
Balance as per nominal ledger	120,000	30,000
Less: Disposal	(30,000)	(5,700)
* £30,000 – £24,300	90,000	24,300

Office equipment

	Cost £	Accumulated depreciation £	Net book value £
Motor vehicles	48,000	12,000	36,000
Plant and machinery	90,000	24,300	65,700
Office equipment	27,500	7,500	20,000
	165,500	43,800	121,700
Revised fixed asset register (£147,500 + £22,660)			170,160
Therefore purchase of office equipment			48,460

(b) **Depreciation for 20X4**

Motor vehicles:

	£
25% × £48,000	12,000
25% × £22,660 × $\frac{3}{12}$	1,416 rounded
	13,416

Plant and machinery:

10% × £90,000   9,000

Office equipment:

10% × £68,460   6,846

ANSWER 6

DIAMOND PLC

Freehold land – cost

20X5		£000	20X6		£000
1 Jan	Balance b/d	1,000	31 Dec	Balance c/d	1,000
		1,000			1,000
20X7					
1 Jan	Balance b/d	1,000			

Freehold buildings – cost

20X5		£000	20X5		£000
1 Jan	Balance b/d	500	31 Dec	Balance c/d	550
8 Oct	Cash	50			
		550			550
20X6					
1 Jan	Balance b/d	550			

Freehold buildings – provision for depreciation

20X5		£000	20X5		£000
31 Dec	Balance c/d	221	1 Jan	Balance b/d	210
			31 Dec	Profit and loss	11
		221			221
20X6			20X6		
31 Dec	Balance c/d	232	1 Jan	Balance b/d	221
			31 Dec	Profit and loss	11
		232			232
			20X7		
			1 Jan	Balance b/d	232

Office equipment – cost

20X5		£000	20X5		£000
1 Jan	Balance b/d	40	10 June	Transfer – disposal	8
10 June	Cash	12	31 Dec	Balance c/d	48
	Transfer – disposal	4			
		56			56
20X6			20X6		
1 Jan	Balance b/d	48	1 Mar	Transfer – disposal	8
			31 Dec	Balance c/d	40
		48			48
20X7					
1 Jan	Balance b/d	40			

Office equipment – provision for depreciation

20X5		£000	20X5		£000
10 June	Transfer – disposal	7	1 Jan	Balance b/d	24
31 Dec	Balance c/d	23	31 Dec	Profit and loss	6
		30			30
20X6			20X6		
1 Mar	Transfer – disposal	6	1 Jan	Balance b/d	23
31 Dec	Balance c/d	22	31 Dec	Profit and loss	5
		28			28
			20X7		
			1 Jan	Balance b/d	22

Office equipment – disposal

20X5		£000	20X5		£000
10 Jun	Office equip. cost	8	10 June	Office equip. deprec.	7
31 Dec	Profit and loss – profit	3		Office equip. – cost	4
		11			11
20X6			20X6		
1 Mar	Office equip. cost	8	1 Mar	Office equip. deprec.	6
31 Dec	Profit and loss – profit	1		Cash – proceeds of sale	3
		9			9

ANSWER 7

A CLIENT

(a) The car was purchased during the year ended 30 April 20X3. Depreciation was charged for the seven months from October 20X2 until the year end, giving a charge for the year of 20% × £15,000 × 7/12 = £1,750.

The car was disposed of during the year ended 30 April 20X4. Depreciation was charged for the six months from May 20X3 until October 20X3, giving a charge for the year of 20% × £15,000 × 6/12 = £1,500.

The accumulated depreciation on the car = £1,750 + £1,500 = £3,250.

(b)

Disposal

	£		£
Motor vehicles – cost	15,000	Motor vehicles – cost (trade in)	10,500
		Motor vehicles – depreciation	3,250
		Profit and loss (loss)	1,250
	15,000		15,000

Note: The question did not require the preparation of a disposal account. It is, however, an efficient way to lay out the working.

(c) The company had vehicles costing £37,200 from May 20X3 until October 20X3. This is a period of six months and depreciation for this period would be 20% × £37,200 × 6/12 = £3,720.

The company had vehicles costing £37,200 – 15,000 + 9,000 + 10,500 = £41,700 from November 20X3 until April 20X4. This is a six-month period for which depreciation would be 20% × £41,700 × 6/12 = £4,170.

Total depreciation for the year = £3,720 + 4,170 = £7,890.

(d)

Motor vehicles at cost

	£		£
Bal b/d	37,200	Disposal	15,000
Loan	9,000		
Disposal (trade in allowance)	10,500	Bal c/d	41,700
	56,700		56,700
Bal b/d	41,700		

ANSWER 8

DEBBIE FRASER

(a) **Depreciation charge is 25% of cost of new car**

	£
Cost of new car is:	
Cheque payment	8,200
Add: Trade in allowance	6,500
	14,700

Depreciation charge = 25% × £14,700 = 3,675

(b) **Calculation of NBV on disposal:**

	£
Original cost @ November 20X0	12,800

Depreciation method is reducing balance

∴ Depreciation charge each year would be:

1st year to 31 October 20X1:

25% × £12,800   3,200

2nd year to 31 October 20X2:

NBV = (£12,800 − £3,200) £9,600

Depreciation charge is 25% × £9,600   2,400

3rd year to 31 October 20X3

NBV = (£12,800 − (£3,200 + £2,400) £7,200

Depreciation charge is nil in year of disposal.

At disposal the NBV was £7,200 and the proceeds were £6,500 (the trade in allowance).

The result being a loss on disposal of £700.

(Proceeds £6,500 − NBV £7,200)

(c) The balance on the disposal account is transferred to the profit and loss account. A profit on disposal is shown as income but a loss (as in this case) is shown on the debit side as an expense.

(d)

Motor vehicles at cost account

	£		£
Balance b/f	12,800	Disposal account (cost)	12,800
Disposal account (trade in)	6,500	Balance c/f (new car)	14,700
Bank (proceeds)	8,200		
	27,500		27,500

(e) The difference between the two methods is as follows:

Straight line method: Depreciation is *calculated on the cost* of the asset, giving a uniform annual rate of depreciation over its life.

Reducing balance method: Depreciation is *calculated on the net book value* of the asset (cost less depreciation charged in previous years), giving a reducing annual rate of depreciation over its life.

ANSWER 9

RAMSEY

Account	Trial balance as at 31.12.20X8 Dr £	Cr £	Adjustments Dr £	Cr £	Trading and profit and loss account Dr £	Cr £	Balance sheet Dr £	Cr £
Capital		24,860						24,860
Sales		94,360				94,360		
Purchases	48,910				48,910			
Fixed assets at cost	32,750						32,750	
Provision for dep'n		11,500		3,275				14,775
Debtors	17,190						17,190	
Bank	18,100						18,100	
Creditors		11,075						11,075
Stock	8,620		9,180	9,180	8,620	9,180	9,180	
Rent	4,200			300	3,900			
Electricity	2,150		250		2,400			
Drawings	9,875						9,875	
Depreciation expense			3,275		3,275			
Prepayments/accruals			300	250			300	250
					67,105	103,540		
Profit for year					36,435			36,435
	141,795	141,795	13,005	13,005	103,540	103,540	87,395	87,395

KAPLAN PUBLISHING 65

ANSWER 10

JANE SIMPSON

(a) **Uncorrected trial balance as at 30 April 20X9**

	£	£
Fixtures and fittings	5,000	
Motor vehicles	4,000	
Stock in trade	12,000	
Trade debtors	7,000	
Balance at bank	1,700	
Trade creditors		6,900
Sales		132,000
Cost of sales	79,200	
Establishment and administrative expenses	11,800	
Sales and distribution expenses	33,500	
Drawings	9,700	
Capital		30,000
	163,900	
Suspense account (bal fig)	5,000	
	168,900	168,900

Tutorial note: Take care to read the requirement. An **uncorrected** trial balance is required.

(b)

Journal

	Dr £	Cr £
Fixtures and fittings	4,500	
Suspense		4,500
Assets purchased but not posted from cash book		
Debtors	500	
Suspense		500
Error in recording sale of £4,700 to debtors		
Drawings	600	
Purchases		600
Goods withdrawn by proprietor for own use		

(c) **Corrected trial balance as at 30 April 20X9**

	£	£
Fixtures and fittings	9,500	
Motor vehicles	4,000	
Stock in trade	12,000	
Trade debtors	7,500	
Balance at bank	1,700	
Trade creditors		6,900
Sales		132,000
Cost of sales	78,600	
Establishment and administrative expenses	11,800	
Sales and distribution expenses	33,500	
Drawings	10,300	
Capital		30,000
	168,900	168,900

ANSWER 11

JEFFREY

(a) (i) Carriage inwards needs to be increased to £1,238 (£974 + £264).

Returns inwards need to be reduced to £111 (£375 – £264).

(ii) Sales need to be reduced to £90,470 (£90,560 – £90).

Debtors need to be reduced to £12,790 (£12,880 – £90).

(iii) Telephone expenses need to be increased to £1,150 (£853 + £297).

Creditors and accruals need to be increased to £6,858 (£6,561 + £297).

(b) (i) **Jeffrey**

Profit and loss account for the year ended 30 September 20X4

	£	£
Sales		90,470
Less: Returns inwards		(111)
		90,359
Cost of sales		
Opening stock	12,560	
Purchases	72,674	
Carriage inwards	1,238	
	86,472	
Less: Closing stock	(11,875)	74,597
Gross profit		15,762
Less: expenses		
Wages	4,684	
Rent	3,200	
Stationery	382	
Travel	749	
Telephone	1,150	
General expenses	753	(10,918)
Net profit		4,844

(ii) The closing capital balance is calculated as follows:

	£
Opening capital	30,217
Net profit	4,844
Less: Drawings	(12,500)
Closing capital	22,561

ANSWER 12

YATTON

(a) **Yatton**

Trading and profit and loss account for year ended 31 December 20X8

	£	£
Sales (*step 3*)		7,850
Cost of sales		
Opening stock	1,400	
Purchases (*step 4*)	3,000	
	4,400	
Less: Closing stock	(1,700)	
		(2,700)
Gross profit		5,150
Expenses (*step 5*)	1,350	
Bad debts (*step 5*)	135	
Depreciation of van (*step 5*)	50	
		(1,535)
Net profit		3,615

(b)

	£
Opening capital (*step 6*)	1,670
Profit for the year (P&L account)	3,615
Drawings (*step 5*)	(2,840)
Closing capital	2,445

Commentary

Step 1 Produce proforma, inserting main headings and certain information such as opening and closing stock. As subsequent steps are completed, insert as many figures in the proformas as possible.

Step 2 Prepare the cash account, and post the cash and bank entries to the other accounts. The question already provides a bank account so this is not required.

Cash

	£		£
Balance b/d	70	Bank	3,000
Bank	200	Purchases control account	400
Debtors control account	5,200	Expenses	500
		Drawings (bal fig)	1,540
		Balance c/d	30
	5,470		5,470

Step 3 Complete the debtors control account. Note the adjustment for bad debts.

Debtors control account

	£		£
Balance b/d	300	Bank	2,500
Trading and profit and loss sales (bal fig)	7,850	Cash	5,200
		Bad debts	100
		Balance c/d (£450 – £100)	350
	8,150		8,150

Tutorial note: Inclusion of the cash sales and purchases in the control accounts will produce a total sales and total purchases figure, rather than credit sales and credit purchases.

Step 4 Complete the creditors control account.

Creditors control account

	£		£
Bank	2,500	Balance b/d	800
Cash	400	Trading and profit and loss	
Balance c/d	900	– purchases (bal fig)	3,000
	3,800		3,800

Step 5 Other adjustments.

Expenses

	£		£
Bank	800	Balance b/d	100
Cash	500	Trading and profit and loss	
Balance c/d	150	(bal fig)	1,35
	1,450		1,450

Drawings

	£		£
Bank	1,300	Capital	2,840
Cash	1,540		
	2,840		2,840

Bad debts

	£		£
Debtors control account	100	Profit and loss	135
Allowance for doubtful debts	35		
	135		135

Allowance for doubtful debts

	£		£
Balance c/d (10% × £350)	35	Balance b/d	Nil
		Bad debts	35
	35		35

Depreciation charge 20% × 3 months × £1,000 = £50

Step 6 Finish the profit and loss account and calculation of capital.

Statement of opening capital

	Dr £	Cr £
Bank	800	
Cash	70	
Debtors	300	
Trade creditors		800
Expense creditors		100
Stock	1,400	
	2,570	900
	900	
	1,670	

Thus debits (assets) exceeds credits (liabilities) by £1,670. Accordingly Yatton's business has net assets of £1,670, represented on the balance sheet by his capital account.

ANSWER 13

TOM WEST

(a) **Capital at 30 June 20X8**

Assets:

Bank as at 30 June 20X8

	Income £	Expenses £	Drawing £	Net £
Year to 30 June 20X6	1,200	(400)	(300)	500
Year to 30 June 20X6	3,500	(1,200)	(1,800)	500
Year to 30 June 20X6	5,700	(2,900)	(2,700)	100
				1,100
Computer as at 30 June 20X8 = £4,500 × 2/5 =				1,800
Debtors as at 30 June 20X8				900
				3,800

Assets = Capital + Liabilities.

There were no liabilities at 30 June 20X8 and so capital = assets = £3,800.

(b) **Tom West**

Profit and loss account for the year ended 30 June 20X9

	£	£
Sales		12,800
Stationery	250	
Motor expenses	790	
Electricity	560	
Repairs	425	
Travel	615	
Depreciation – computer	900	
Depreciation – office furniture	140	
		3,680
		9,120

Working for sales

Debtors

		£			£
1 July 20X8 Bal b/d		900	Bank		11,000
Balancing fig. Sales		12,800	30 June 20X9 Bal c/d		2,700
		13,700			13,700
1 July 20X9 Bal b/d		2,700			

(c) **Tom West**

Capital at 30 June 20X9

Capital

Balance as at 30 June 20X8	3,800
Invested during year	3,000
Profit for year	9,120
	15,920
Drawings	4,600
	11,320

ANSWER 14

SIMON MEREDITH

(a)

Debtors control account

		£		£
	Opening balance	29,720	Cash (W1)	273,000
Bal fig	Sales	274,780	Closing balance	31,500
		304,500		304,500

(W1)	Cash received	£298,000
	Less Capital introduced	£25,000
		£273,000

(b)

	£	£
Sales (i)		274,780
Cost of sales		
Opening stock	16,800	
Purchases (W2)	236,100	
	252,900	
Closing stock	17,500	235,400
Gross profit		39,380

(W2)

Creditors control account

	£		£
Paid (W3)	237,300	Opening balance	23,900
Closing balance	22,700	Purchases (bal fig)	236,100
	260,000		260,000

(W3)

	£	£
Cheques issued		295,300
Less: Expenses	32,000	
New van	11,000	
Drawings	15,000	
		58,000
		237,300

ANSWER 15

J PATEL

Balance sheet as at 31 October 20X9

	Cost £	depreciation £	£
Fixed assets			
Fixtures and fittings	10,000	(7,000)	3,000
Motor vehicles	20,200	(4,720)	15,480
	30,200	(11,720)	18,480
Current assets			
Stock		23,700	
Trade debtors (W1)		11,500	
Balance at bank (W4)		6,620	
Cash in hand		200	
		42,020	
Current liabilities			
Trade creditors (W3)		(12,700)	
			29,320
			47,800
Capital – At 1 November 20X8			30,910
Add: New capital – proceeds of sale of land			16,000
Net profit for year			12,530
Drawings (£8,500 + 3,140 (W2))			(11,640)
			47,800

Workings

(W1) **Total debtors account**

	£		£
Balance b/d	19,630	Cash banked from credit sales	181,370
Credit sales	173,770	Bad debts written off	530
		Balance c/d (bal fig)	11,500
	193,400		193,400

(W2)

Cash

	£		£
Balance b/d	160	Bankings	61,190
Cash from cash sales	64,370	Drawings (bal fig)	3,140
(total sales – credit sales)		Balance c/d	200
(238,140 – 173,770)			
	64,530		64,530

(W3)

Total creditors account

	£		£
Cash paid (per bank)	163,100	Balance b/d	9,440
Balance c/d (bal fig)	12,700	Purchases	166,360
	175,800		175,800

(W4)

Bank

	£		£
Receipts	258,560	Balance b/d	6,740
		Payments	245,200
		Balance c/d	6,620
	258,560		258,560

ANSWER 16

R THOMAS

(a) **Trading and profit and loss account for the year ended 31 May 20X9**

		£000	£000
Sales (W1)			1,270
Less: Cost of sales			
Opening stock		150	
Purchases (W2)		635	
		785	
Less: Closing stock		190	
			595
Gross profit			675
Less: Expenses			
Insurance (25 + 15)		40	
Rent (40 + 12 – 10)		42	
Rates		5	
Electricity (30 – 6 + 15)		39	
Telephone (14 – 4 – 1)		9	
Motor vehicle expenses		20	
Wages		120	
Depreciation:			
Vehicles (25% × 100)		25	
Equipment (20% × (200 – 80))		24	
Discounts allowed		30	
Irrecoverable debts written off		35	
			389
Net profit			286

(b) **Balance sheet as at 31 May 20X9**

	Cost £000	Accumulated depreciation £000	NBV £000
Fixed assets:			
Vehicles	100	75	25
Equipment	200	104	96
			121
Current assets:			
Stock		190	
Debtors		230	
Prepayments (10 + 1)		11	
Bank (W3)		224	
		655	
Creditors: amounts falling due within one year			
Creditors		155	
Accruals		15	
		170	
Net current assets			485
			606
Proprietor's capital: Opening capital			420
Add: Profit for the year			286
			706
Less: Drawings			100
			606

Workings

(W1) **Debtors control account**

	£000		£000
Opening balance	225	Receipts	1,200
		Irrecoverable debts	35
		Discounts	30
Sales	1,270	Closing balance	230
	1,495		1,495

(W2)

Creditors control account

	£000		£000
Payments	650	Opening balance	170
Closing balance	155	Purchases	635
	805		805

(W3) **Bank account**

	£000		£000
Opening balance	28	Creditors	650
Debtors	1,200	Insurance	25
		Rent	40
		Rates	5
		Electricity	30
		Telephone	14
		Motor vehicle expenses	20
		Wages	120
		Drawings	100
		Closing balance	224
	1,228		1,228

ANSWER 17

AMBER, BERYL AND CORAL

(a) **Trading and profit and loss account for the year ended 31 December 20X6**

		£	£
Sales			2,000,000
Less: Cost of sales			
Opening stock		180,000	
Purchases		1,400,000	
		1,580,000	
Less: Closing stock		(200,000)	
			(1,380,000)
Gross profit			620,000
Expenses			
Wages and salaries (228,000 + 12,000)		240,000	
Sundry expenses		120,000	
Bad and doubtful debts (16,000 + 10,000)		26,000	
Depreciation:			
Building (2% × 250,000)		5,000	
Plant and equipment (10% × 240,000)		24,000	
Interest on loan – Amber (10% × 50,000)		5,000	
			(420,000)
Net profit			200,000

Profit and loss appropriation account

	Amber £	Beryl £	Coral £	Total £
1.1.X6 to 30.6.X6				
Salaries	10,000	10,000		20,000
Share of profit:				
£80,000 divided 60:40	48,000	32,000		80,000
1.7.X6 to 31.12.X6				
£100,000 divided 40:40:20	40,000	40,000	20,000	100,000
	98,000	82,000	20,000	200,000

Balance sheet as at 31 December 20X6

	Cost or valuation £	Aggregate depreciation £	Net book value £
Fixed assets			
Land at valuation	280,000	Nil	280,000
Buildings	250,000	35,000	215,000
Plant, equipment and vehicles	240,000	74,000	166,000
	770,000	109,000	661,000

Current assets			
Stock		200,000	
Debtors (420,000 – 16,000)	404,000		
Less: Allowance for doubtful debts (20,000 + 10,000)	30,000		
		374,000	
Cash at bank		38,000	
		612,000	
Less: Current liabilities			
Creditors – trade	350,000		
bonus	12,000		
		(362,000)	250,000
			911,000
Loan – Amber			(50,000)
			861,000

Capital accounts	Amber	368,000	
	Beryl	242,000	
	Coral	100,000	
			710,000
Current accounts	Amber	82,000	
	Beryl	64,000	
	Coral	5,000	
			151,000
			861,000

(b)

Partners' capital accounts

	A £	B £	C £		A £	B £	C £
Goodwill	80,000	80,000	40,000	Balance b/d	280,000	210,000	
Balances c/d	368,000	242,000	100,000	Cash			140,000
				Goodwill (W)	120,000	80,000	
				Revaluation	48,000	32,000	
	448,000	322,000	140,000		448,000	322,000	140,000

Partners' current accounts

	A £	B £	C £		A £	B £	C £
Drawings	28,000	24,000	15,000	Balance b/d	7,000	6,000	
Balances c/d	82,000	64,000	5,000	Profit for year	98,000	82,000	20,000
				Loan interest	5,000		
	110,000	88,000	20,000		110,000	88,000	20,000

Working

Goodwill = $\frac{100}{20} \times £40,000 = £200,000$

ANSWER 18

SMITH, JONES AND MATTHEWS

(a) **Trading and profit and loss account for the year ended 30 September 20X8**

		£	£
Sales			736,750
Returns inwards			(23,800)
			712,950
Less: Cost of sales			
Opening stock		149,975	
Purchases		480,165	
Carriage inwards		5,250	
		635,390	
Less: Closing stock		(178,710)	
			456,680
Gross profit			256,270
Less: Expenses			
Discounts allowed		385	
Irrecoverable debts (W1)		4,564	
General expenses		3,308	
Rent and rates (8,978 – 420)		8,558	
Postages		8,575	
Motor expenses		13,790	
Salaries and wages		64,036	
Depreciation:			
Motor vans		8,750	
Office equipment		5,880	
			117,846
Net profit before appropriations			138,424
Add: Interest on drawings			
Smith		595	
Jones		385	
Matthews		420	
			1,400
			139,824
Less: Salaries			
Smith		4,200	
Jones		2,450	
Matthews		3,500	
			10,150
			129,674

KAPLAN PUBLISHING   83

		£	£
Interest on capital			
Smith (10% × 105,000)		10,500	
Jones (10% × 56,000)		5,600	
Matthews (10% × 42,000)		4,200	
			(20,300)
			109,374
Profits shared:			
Smith (109,374 × 6/12)		54,687	
Jones (109,374 × 4/12)		36,458	
Matthews (109,374 × 2/12)		18,229	
			109,374

(b) **Partners' current accounts**

	Smith £	Jones £	Matthews £		Smith £	Jones £	Matthews £
Balance b/d			536	Balance b/d	7,260	4,865	
Interest on drawings	595	385	420	Salaries	4,200	2,450	3,500
Drawings	44,135	29,460	21,756	Interest on capital	10,500	5,600	4,200
Balance c/d	31,917	19,528	3,217	Profit share	54,687	36,458	18,229
	76,647	49,373	25,929		76,647	49,373	25,929

(c) **Balance sheet as at 30 September 20X8**

	Cost £	Accumulated depreciation £	Net book value £
Fixed assets:			
Motor vans	43,750		
(14,700 + 8,750)		23,450	20,300
Office equipment	29,400		
(9,450 + 5,880)		15,330	14,070
			34,370
Current assets:			
Stock		178,710	
Debtors (130,123 – 3,045)		127,078	
Prepayments		420	
Cash at bank		2,330	
		308,538	
Creditors: amounts falling due within one year		85,246	
			223,292
			257,662

Financed by:
Capital accounts:

Smith		105,000
Jones		56,000
Matthews		42,000
		203,000

Current accounts:

Smith	31,917	
Jones	19,528	
Matthews	3,217	
		54,662
		257,662

Working

(W1) **Irrecoverable debts**

	£
Per trial balance	4,319
Increase in provision (3,045 – 2,800)	245
	4,564

ANSWER 19

CAIN AND ABEL

(a) (i) **Cain and Abel**

Trading and profit and loss account for the year ended 31 October 20X0

	£	£
Sales		1,483,400
Opening stock	195,300	
Add: Purchases	1,143,400	
	1,338,700	
Less: Closing stock	296,700	
Cost of goods sold		1,042,000
Gross profit		441,400
Expenses		
Office expenses	72,000	
Rent	9,000	
Insurance (8,650 – 850)	7,800	
Motor vehicle expenses (44,500 – 5,000)	39,500	
Discounts allowed	28,800	
Wages and salaries (82,000 + 3,475)	86,275	
Depreciation – Vans (90,000 – 66,600) × 20%	4,680	
– Fittings (28,000 – 12,800) × 10%	1,520	
– Motor car (18,000 × 20%/2)	1,800	
Bank charges	655	
Irrecoverable debts (2,200 + 6,750 – 6,000)	2,950	
		254,980
		186,420

Appropriation account

	Cain £	Abel £	£
Profit for year			186,420
Add: Interest on drawings	(2,400)	(1,420)	3,820
			190,240
Less: Interest on capital	15,400	13,800	(29,200)
			161,040
Balance in profit sharing ratio 3:2	96,624	64,416	(161,040)
	109,624	76,796	–

(ii) **Current accounts**

Cain

	£		£
Drawings	40,000	Interest on capital	15,400
Interest on drawings	2,400	Share of profit	96,624
Balance c/f	69,624		
	112,024		112,024

Abel

	£		£
Drawings	27,000	Interest on capital	13,800
Motor vehicle exps (1,800 + 5,000)	6,800	Share of profit	64,416
Interest on drawings	1,420		
Balance c/f	42,996		
	78,216		78,216

(iii) **Cain and Abel**

Balance sheet as at 31 October 20X0

	Cost £	Accumulated depreciation £	Net book value £
Fixed assets			
Fittings	28,000	14,320	13,680
Vans	90,000	71,280	18,720
Motor car	18,000	3,600	14,400
	136,000	89,200	46,800
Current assets			
Stock		296,700	
Debtors (137,200 – 2,200)	135,000		
Less: Allowance for doubtful debts	6,750	128,250	
Prepayment – insurance		850	
		425,800	
Current liabilities			
Creditors	47,200		
Bank overdrafts (7,650 + 655)	8,305		
Accruals (3,745 + 9,000)	12,475		
		67,980	
Net current assets			357,820
			404,620

Capital accounts

Cain	154,000	
Abel	138,000	292,000

Current accounts (per (a)(ii))

Cain	69,624	
Abel	42,996	112,620
		404,620

(b) **Advantages of a partnership over a sole trader:**

(i) Capital can be raised from more than one person, facilitating expansion.

(ii) Partners may contribute special skills not easily combined in a single person.

(iii) Financial risk is shared among several people.

(iv) A greater number of business contacts may be available.

Disadvantages of a partnership over sole trader:

(i) There may be disputes among partners as to the policy of the business or the treatment of individual problems.

(ii) Personal problems may develop between partners.

(iii) Liability for partnership's debts is joint and several in England and Wales.

(iv) Inequities in profit sharing may arise or be perceived by partners.

ANSWER 20

JACK AND JILL

(a) **Adjustment to partnership ratio**

Partners	Original ratio	Adjustment	New ratio
Jack	2/3	less 2/3 × 1/6	10/18
Jill	1/3	less 1/3 × 1/6	5/18
Jean	–		3/18

(b) **Capital accounts**

	Jack £000	Jill £000	Jean £000		Jack £000	Jill £000	Jean £000
Goodwill – new ratio	100	50	30	Bal b/f	250	100	–
Balance c/f	270	110	40	Cash introduced	–	–	70
				Goodwill – old ratio	120	60	–
	370	160	70		370	160	70

(c) **Jack, Jill and Jean:** *Workings* **(£000)**

Trading and profit and loss account for the year ended 31 May 20X3

	£000	£000	*Workings*
Sales		979	
Stock at 1 June 20X2	190		
Add: Purchases	725		
	915		
Stock at 31 May 20X3	214		
Cost of goods sold		701	
Gross profit		278	
Expenses			
Rent and insurance	32		(33 – 1)
Sales commission	20		(18 + 2)
Advertising and other expenses	52		
Discounts allowed	25		
Irrecoverable debts	7		
Depreciation – fittings	15		(210 – 60) × 10%
– vehicles	28	179	(180 – 40) × 20%)
Net profit before appropriation		99	
Interest on capital: Jack	15		(Working (i))
Jill	6		(Working (i))
Jean	1	22	(Working (i))
		77	

KAPLAN PUBLISHING

Share of profit:	Jack	49
	Jill	24
	Jean	4
		77

Workings

(i)   **Appropriation of profit for the year ended 31 May 20X3**

		8 months to 31/01/X3 £000	4 months to 31/05/X3 £000	Total for year to 31/05/X3 £000
Profit allocated	8:4	66	33	99
Interest on capital:	Jack	(10)	(5)	(15)
	Jill	(4)	(2)	(6)
	Jean	–	(1)	(1)
		52	25	77
Profit share:	Jack	35	14	49
	Jill	17	7	24
	Jean	–	4	4
		52	25	77

(d)   **Current accounts for the year ended 31 May 20X3**

	Jack £000	Jill £000	Jean £000		Jack £000	Jill £000	Jean £000
Bal b/f	–	15	–	Bal b/f	12	–	–
Drawings	25	10	2	Interest to 31/01/X3	10	4	–
				Interest after 31/01/X3	5	2	1
				Profit to 31/01/X3	35	17	–
Balance c/f	51	5	3	Profit after 31/01/X3	14	7	4
	76	30	5		76	30	5

(e) **Jack, Jill and Jean – Balance sheet as at 31 May 20X3**

	Cost £000	Accumulated depreciation £000	Net book value £000	*Workings*
Fixed assets				
Fittings	210	75	135	
Vehicles	180	68	112	
	390	143	247	
Current assets				
Stock		214		
Debtors		140		
Prepayment – insurance		1		
Cash and bank		33		
		388		
Current liabilities				
Creditors	154			
Accruals	2	156		
Net current assets			232	
			479	
Capital accounts				
Jack		270		(See part (b))
Jill		110		(See part (b))
Jean		40	420	(See part (b))
Current accounts				
Jack		51		(See part (d))
Jill		5		(See part (d))
Jean		3	59	(See part (d))
			479	

ANSWER 21

LINCOLN PLC

Lincoln plc

Profit and loss account for the year ended 31 December 20X9

	£000	£000	£000
Sales			5,000
Less: Returns			(100)
			4,900
Less: Cost of goods sold			
Opening stock		300	
Purchases	2,400		
Less: Returns	(150)		
Less: Stock taken for private use	(10)		
		2,240	
		2,540	
Closing stock		(400)	
			(2,140)
Gross profit			2,760
Operating expenses			
Figure given	1,300		
Property depreciation	16		
Machinery depreciation	108		
Cash discounts (20 – 10)	10		
			(1,434)
Net operating profit			1,326
Payment for injury	50		
Debenture interest paid and proposed	90		
Less: Gain on redemption	(20)		
			(120)
Net profit			1,206

Lincoln plc

Balance sheet as at 31 December 20X9

	Cost/valuation £000	Depreciation £000	Net £000
Fixed assets			
Land	1,500	Nil	1,500
Property	800	216	584
Machinery	1,600	608	992
			3,076
Current assets			
Stock		400	
Debtors		1,000	
Due from director		10	
		1,410	
Current liabilities			
Creditors	400		
Debenture interest	30		
Bank overdraft	30		
		(460)	
Net current assets			950
Long-term liabilities			
Debentures (15%)			(400)
Net assets			3,626
Represented by			
Share capital			1,100
Share premium			620
Revaluation reserve			600
Profit and loss account reserves (200 + 1,206 – 100)			1,306
			3,626

Workings

(W1)

Suspense account

	£000		£000
B/f	210	Redemption of debentures	380
Share issue	220	Payment – injury	50
	430		430

(W2) **Depreciation**

Machinery	Cost £000	Depreciation £000
Balance per question	1,600	500
Depreciated to scrap value	(160)	(150)
	1,440	350

Remaining net book value	1,090
Scrap value – not to be depreciated	(10)
	1,080

ANSWER 22

BOWDERRY CO LTD

(a) **Profit and loss account for the year ended 31 May 20X8**

	£	£
Sales		500,000
Returns inwards		(2,732)
		497,268
Opening stock	91,788	
Purchases	264,636	
	356,424	
Closing stock	(95,500)	
		(260,924)
Gross profit		236,344
Discounts received		12,400
		248,744
Rates	15,000	
Wages and salaries (50,000 + 1,900)	51,900	
Insurance (12,500 – 700)	11,800	
General expenses	3,120	
Irrecoverable debts (W1)	3,667	
Depreciation (W2)	40,000	
		(125,487)
Operating profit		123,257
Debenture interest (4,800 + 4,800)		(9,600)
Preference dividends (3,900 + 3,900)		(7,800)
Profit before tax		105,857
Taxation		(40,000)
Profit after tax		65,857

KAPLAN PUBLISHING

(b) **Balance sheet at 31 May 20X8**

	£	£	£
Fixed assets:			
Land		206,400	
Buildings (W2)		180,000	
Furniture and fittings (W2)		64,000	
			450,400
Current assets:			
Stocks		95,500	
Debtors (96,140 – 4,807 (W1))		91,333	
Prepayments		700	
Cash in hand		1,424	
		188,957	
Creditors: amounts falling due within one year:			
Bank overdraft	49,100		
Creditors	39,800		
Corporation tax	40,000		
Dividends proposed	19,500		
Accruals (1,900 + 4,800)	6,700		
		(155,100)	
Net current assets			33,857
Total assets less current liabilities			484,257
Creditors: amounts falling due after more than one year:			
10% Debentures			(96,000)
6% £1 preference shares			(130,000)
			258,257
Capital and reserves:			
Called up share capital: Ordinary shares			130,000
Share premium			6,000
Fixed asset replacement reserve (60,000 + 30,000)			90,000
Profit and loss account (W3)			32,257
			258,257

Workings

(W1) **Irrecoverable debts**

	£
Provision b/f	5,196
Less: Provision required (96,140 × 5%)	(4,807)
Profit and loss account (credit)	(389)
Add: Bad debt expense	4,056
	3,667

(W2) **Depreciation**

	Land £	Buildings £	Furniture and fittings £
Cost	206,400	240,000	140,000
Depreciation b/f	–	36,000	60,000
Charge for year (240,000 × 10%)	–	24,000	
Charge for year (140,000 – 60,000) × 20%	–		16,000
Depreciation c/f	–	60,000	76,000
Net book value c/f	206,400	180,000	64,000

(W3) **Profit and loss account**

	£
At 1 June 20X7	12,000
Profit for the year	65,857
Transfer to fixed asset replacement reserve	(30,000)
Dividends	(15,600)
At 31 May 20X8	32,257

ANSWER 23

ARNFIELD LTD

(a) **Profit and loss account for the year ended 31 October 20X9**

	£000	£000
Sales		7,900
Returns		30
		7,870
Opening stock	700	
Add purchases	3,500	
	4,200	
Less closing stock	900	
Cost of sales		3,300
Gross profit		4,570
Discounts received		130
		4,700
Rates	100	
Advertising (W1)	20	
Insurance	70	
Wages and salaries (W2)	820	
Heating and lighting	80	
General expenses	20	
Telephone	40	
Bad debts (W3)	610	
Depreciation – Building	200	
– Motor vehicles	10	
– Furniture and equipment	130	
		2,100
Operating profit		2,600
Finance costs		
Preference dividend	18	
Debenture interest	50	
		68
Profit before tax		2,532
Corporation tax		700
Net profit after tax		1,832
Transfer to fixed assets reserve		150
Profit retained for the year		1,682
Profit and loss account b/f		100
Profit and loss account c/f		1,782

(b) **Balance sheet as at 31 October, 20X9**

	Cost/ valuation £000	Accumulated depreciation £000	Net book value £000
Fixed assets			
Land	600	–	600
Buildings	2,300	–	2,300
Fixtures and equipment	1,000 (W4)	480	520
Motor vehicles	70 (W5)	30	40
	3,970	510	3,460
Current assets			
Stock		900	
Debtors	1,960		
Less allowance for doubtful debts	50	1,910	
Prepayments		10	
Cash in hand		140	
		2,960	
Creditors amounts falling due within one year			
Bank overdraft	300		
Trade creditors	320		
Corporation tax	700		
Accruals	70		
Dividends	18		
		1,408	
Net current assets			1,552
Total assets less current liabilities			5,012
Creditors amounts falling due after more that one year			
10% Debentures			(500)
6% £1 preference shares			(300)
			4,212
Capital and reserves			
Called up share capital:			
£1 Ordinary shares			1,240
Share premium account			40
Revaluation reserve (W6)			900
Fixed asset replacement reserve			250
Profit and loss account (100 + 1,832 – 150)			1,782
			4,212

Workings

(W1) Advertising

	£000		£000
		Profit and loss account	20
Balance per TB	30	Prepayment c/d	10
	30		30
Prepayment b/d	10		

(W2) Wages and salaries

	£000		£000
Balance per TB	750	Profit and loss account	820
Accrued exps c/d	70		
	820		820
		Accrued exps b/d	70

(W3) Allowance for doubtful debts

	£000		£000
Balance c/d	50	Balance per TB	40
		Irrecoverable debts	
		(increase in provision)	10
	50		50
		Balance b/d	50

Irrecoverable debts

	£000		£000
Balance per TB	600	Profit and loss account	610
From allowance for doubtful debts	10		
	610		610

(W4) Accumulated depreciation – Furniture and equipment

	£000		£000
Balance c/d	480	Balance per TB	350
		Charge for year	
		(20% × £650,000)	130
	480		480
		Balance b/d	480

(W5) **Accumulated depreciation – Motor vehicles**

	£000		£000
Balance c/d	30	Balance per TB	20
		Charge for year	
		(20% × £650,000)	10
	30		30
		Balance b/d	30

(W6) **Revaluation reserve**

Buildings   £000

As per trial balance:
Cost   2,000
Accumulated depreciation   400
                                                                         1,600
Depreciation charge for year   200

Net book value before revaluation   1,400
Revaluation at 31 October 20X9   2,300

Increase in valuation over net book value   900

Increase requests a revaluation reserve of £900,000.

KAPLAN PUBLISHING   101

ANSWER 24

MUGGERIDGE LTD

(a) (i) **Muggeridge Ltd**

Profit and loss account for the year ended 31 December 20X9

	£000	£000
Sales		3,000
Opening stock	450	
Purchases (W1)	1,940	
Carriage inwards	90	
	2,480	
Less closing stock	500	
Cost of sales		1,980
Gross profit		1,020
Discount received		70
		1,090
Discount allowed	60	
Wages (W2)	245	
Directors' remuneration	50	
Heating and lighting	230	
Other expenses	50	
Depreciation (W3)	175	
Increase in allowance for doubtful debts (W4)	5	
Amortised goodwill	10	
		825
Net profit before interest and tax		265
Debenture interest		50
Preference dividend		35
Net profit before tax		265
Corporation tax		55
Net profit after tax		125

Workings

(W1) **Purchases**

	£000
Per trial balance	1,900
Absorbed on 1 January, 20X9	40
To profit and loss account	1,940

(W2) **Wages**

	£000
Per trial balance	215
Accrued wages	30
	245

(W3) **Depreciation**

Depreciation – buildings

	£000		£000
Balance c/d	180	Balance b/d	135
		Charge for year (5% × £900)	45
	180		180
		Balance b/d	180

Depreciation – plant

	£000		£000
Balance c/d	500	Balance b/d	370
		Charge for year (20% × 1,020 – 370)	130
	500		500
		Balance b/d	500

Depreciation charges

	£000		£000
Buildings	45	Profit and loss account	175
Plant	130		
	175		175

(W4) **Allowance for doubtful debts**

	£000		£000
Balance c/d (5% × 600 (debtors))	30	Balance b/d	25
		Profit and loss account	5
	30		30
		Balance b/d	30

(ii) **Muggeridge Ltd – Balance sheet as at 31 December 20X9**

	Cost £000	Accumulated depreciation £000	Net book value £000
Fixed assets			
Intangible assets			
Goodwill	100	10	90
Tangible assets			
Land	300	–	300
Buildings	900	180	720
Plant	1,020	500	520
	2,220	680	1,540
			1,630
Current assets			
Stock		500	
Debtors	600		
Less allowance for doubtful debts	30		
		570	
Bank		135	
		1,205	
Creditors: amounts falling due within one year			
Trade creditors	900		
Corporation tax	55		
Accruals	80		
Preference dividend accrued	35		
		1,070	
Net current assets			135
Total assets less current liabilities			1,765
Creditors: amounts falling due after more than one year			
10% debentures			(500)
7% preference shares of 50p			(500)
			765
Capital and reserves			
Called up share capital ordinary shares of £1			490
Share premium account			80
Fixed asset replacement reserve			50
Profit and loss account (40 + 125 – 20)			145
			765

(b) **Bonus (scrip) issue**

Definition: The issue of bonus shares represents the issue of shares to existing shareholders in proportion to their existing holdings.

The issue is funded totally by the reserves held by the issuing company. Non-distributable reserves, such as share premium account, would ideally be used first for the funding of the issue followed by other reserves, such as capital redemption reserve, and the balance retained on the profit and loss account.

When a company makes a bonus issue, it is often regarded as a show of strength by that company; a positive move which often reflects in a fall in the market price per share thus attracting more investors.

A bonus issue is really a paper exercise which moves funds from reserves into equity share capital.

The effect is to increase the number of shares issued, spreading the ownership, whilst offering creditors greater protection and encouraging new investors to buy the shares as they become available. By increasing the share capital, this often brings the share capital more into line with the fixed assets of the company, creating a better balance of fixed assets to share equity.

ANSWER 25

RP ATTON LTD

Tutorial note:

Although RP Atton is a limited company, the financial statements are being prepared for internal use. Therefore, the P&L will detail the cost of sales and expenses, rather than just displaying the totals for cost of sales, selling and distribution costs, and administrative expenses as required by the Companies Act.

Likewise, the face of the balance sheet will also show more detail.

The skills being tested by this question are basically those covered by your earlier studies of sole traders. The key differences are that tax and dividends will be charged through the P&L and recognised as liabilities in the balance sheet. Don't forget the accrual for the preference dividends.

(a) **RP Atton Ltd**
Trading and profit and loss account for the year ended 31 May 20X3

		£000	£000
Sales			8,500
Less returns inwards			(85)
Turnover			8,415
Cost of sales			
Opening stock		650	
Purchases		3,300	
Less: Closing stock		(500)	
Cost of sales			(3,450)
Gross profit			4,965
Expenses			
Depreciation			
Buildings	*2,500 × 5%*	125	
Motor vehicles	*(160 – 60) × 20%*	20	
Furniture and equipment	*1,500 × 20%*	300	
General expenses		25	
Insurance	*45 – 11 prepayment*	34	
Advertising		35	
Wages & salaries	*800 + 65 accrual*	865	
Heating and lighting		70	
Telephone		25	
Business rates		75	
Irrecoverable debts		500	
Increase in debt allowance	(W1)	35	
Discounts received		(100)	
			(2,009)
Operating profit			2,956
Finance costs			
Debenture interest			(40)
Preference dividend	*(9% × 200)*		(18)
Profit before tax			2,898
Taxation			(500)
Profit after tax			2,398

KAPLAN PUBLISHING

(b) **RP Atton Ltd**

Balance sheet as at 31 May 20X3

		£000	£000	£000
Tangible fixed assets	Note 1			4,230
Current assets				
Stocks			500	
Debtors *(1,400 – 70)*			1,330	
Prepayments *(Insurance)*			11	
Bank			10	
			1,851	
Current liabilities				
Bank overdraft		123		
Creditors		310		
Accruals *(Wages and salaries)*		65		
Accrued preference dividend		18		
Tax		500		
			(1,016)	
Net current assets				835
Total assets less current liabilities				5,065
8% debenture				(500)
9% £1 preference shares				(200)
Net assets				4,365
Capital and reserves				
£1 ordinary shares	Note 2			1,100
Share premium	Note 2			20
Fixed asset replacement reserve	Note 2			300
Revaluation reserve	Note 2			655
Profit and loss account	Note 2			2,290
Equity shareholders' funds				4,365

Note 1 Tangible fixed assets

	Land £000	Buildings £000	Motor vehicles £000	Furniture & equipment £000	Total £000
Cost					
From TB	550	2,500	160	1,500	4,710
Revaluation	–	200	–	–	200
Closing	550	2,700	160	1,500	4,910
Depreciation					
Opening	–	330	60	300	690
Charge for the year	–	125	20	300	445
Revaluation	–	(455)	–	–	(455)
Closing	–	–	80	600	680
Net book value	550	2,700	80	900	4,230

Note 2 Equity shareholders' funds

	Ordinary shares £000	Share premium £000	Replacement reserve £000	Revaluation reserve £000	P&L account £000	Total £000
Opening bal	1,000	120	50	–	142	1,312
Retained profit	–	–	–	–	2,398	2,398
Revaluation	–	–	–	655*	–	655
Transfer	–	–	250	–	(250)	–
Bonus issue	100	(100)	–	–	–	–
Closing bal	1,100	20	300	655	2,290	4,365

*Revaluation: Increase in 'cost' 200 + Adjustment to depreciation 455.

Working

(W1) Doubtful debt allowance

	£000
Closing allowance: (1,400 × 5%)	70
Less opening allowance from the TB	(35)
Increase charged to the P&L	35

ANSWER 26

POLLARD LTD

(a) (i) **Pollard Limited**

Trading and profit and loss account for the year ended 31 October 20X1

	£000	£000	£000
Sales			4,370
Less: Cost of sales			
Opening stock		600	
Purchases		2,600	
Carriage inwards		170	
		3,370	
Less: Closing stock		450	
			2,920
Gross profit			1,450
Expenses			
Wages (325 + 50)		375	
Directors' fees		100	
Heating and lighting		85	
Insurance (45 – 10)		35	
Other expenses		30	
Audit fee		55	
Discounts allowed		50	
Discounts received		(60)	
Depreciation: building	40		
plant	240	280	
Doubtful debts		85	1,035
Net profit before interest and tax			415
Debenture interest			64
Preference dividends		21	
Net profit before tax			330
Taxation			40
Profit for the year			290

(ii) **Pollard Limited**

Balance sheet as at 31 October 20X1

	Cost £000	Accumulated depreciation £000	Net book value £000
Fixed assets			
Land	400	–	400
Buildings	800	160	640
Plant	1,400	440	960
	2,600	600	2,000

Current assets			
Stock		450	
Debtors	900		
Less provision for doubtful debts	135		
		765	
Prepayments		10	
		1,225	
Less: Current liabilities			
Bank overdraft		75	
Trade creditors		450	
Taxation		40	
Accruals (55 + 50 + 64)		169	
Accrued preference dividend		21	
		755	
			470
			2,470

Less: Net current assets		
Non-current liabilities		
8% debentures		800
7% preference shares of £1 each		300
		1,370

Capital and reserves		
Ordinary shares of £1 each (700 + 140)		840
Share premium account (200 – 140)		60
Fixed asset replacement reserve		100
Profit and loss account (80 + 290)		370
		1,370

(b) (2) Accruals or matching concept.

(3) Accruals concept and prudence concept.

(6) Accruals concept.

(c) **Relevance**

According to the ASB's *Statement of Principles for Financial Reporting*, information is relevant if it has the ability to influence the economic decisions of users and is provided in time to influence those decisions.

Reliability

Financial information is reliable if:

- it represents faithfully what it purports to represent or could reasonably be expected to represent

- it is free from bias (neutral)

- it is free from material error

- it is complete

- a degree of caution has been applied in exercising judgements and making the necessary estimation in conditions of uncertainty.

ANSWER 27

LEWIS LTD AND GORDON LTD

(a) **Method of calculation of ratios**

    (i) **Gross profit percentage**

$$\frac{\text{Gross profit}}{\text{Sales}} \times 100$$

    (ii) **Net profit percentage**

$$\frac{\text{Net profit}}{\text{Sales}} \times 100$$

    (iii) **Return on capital employed**

$$\frac{\text{Net profit before interest}}{\text{Loan capital and share capital and reserves}} \times 100$$

    (iv) **Stock turnover**

$$\frac{\text{Average stock}}{\text{Cost of sales}} \times 365 = \text{Number of days' sales in stock}$$

OR

$$\frac{\text{Cost of sales}}{\text{Average stock}} = \text{Number of times stock is turned over}$$

    (v) **Average settlement period for debtors**

$$\frac{\text{Trade debtors}}{\text{Credit sales}} \times 365$$

    (vi) **Average settlement period for creditors**

$$\frac{\text{Trade creditors}}{\text{Credit purchases}} \times 365$$

(b) (i) **Gross and net profit ratios**

Probably the most important differences between the two companies are picked up by these two ratios. Gordon Ltd somehow manages a 30% gross profit against Lewis's 18%, despite the fact that the companies operate in a similar market selling similar products. One possible explanation is that Lewis's overhead expenses are much higher, evidenced by the fact that the two companies' net profit percentages are the same. If these high overhead expenses are the result of heavy sales promotion spending, that could explain the situation. If this is not the case, Gordon should take steps to control and reduce its expenses, while Lewis should try to increase its margins, possibly by negotiating lower prices from its supplier.

    (ii) **Return on capital employed**

The companies' returns on capital employed are broadly comparable. This ratio is very dependent upon companies' accounting policies and the extent to which their fixed assets have been revalued. More information on these points is necessary before any conclusions can be drawn.

(iii) **Stock turnover**

Gordon turns over its stock in about twice the time taken by Lewis. This could relate to the different rates of gross profit percentage – perhaps Lewis goes for competitively priced items to get a fast turnover of goods, while Gordon tries for higher prices and accepts in return a slower rate of stock turnover.

(iv) **Debtors settlement period**

Gordon's 67 days is a completely acceptable debtor's settlement period, yet somehow Lewis manages to achieve 23 days. Perhaps Lewis offers heavy settlement discounts which are charged in the cost of sales.

(v) **Creditors settlement period**

Both companies settle their creditors promptly. However, Lewis does so without putting strain on its cash position, because its debtors pay so promptly, whilst Gordon on the other hand pays its creditors more quickly than its debtors, thus necessitating a greater amount of working capital.

(c) **Further information**

(i) Current and previous years' financial statements.

(ii) Details of previous years' ratios to reveal trends.

(iii) Industry average figures to provide comparisons.

(iv) Accounting policies of the two companies.

(v) Details of asset revaluations, if any.

(vi) Type of goods sold, market shares and volume of sales.

(vii) National and, if relevant, international market conditions.

(viii) Level of orders and enquiries coming in.

ANSWER 28

G PADGETT

G Padgett
Trading and profit and loss account for the year ended 31 October 20X1

	Workings	£	£
Sales	(W3)		77,500
Less: Cost of sales	(W7)		45,000
Gross profit			32,500
Less: Expenses			
General expenses	(W8)	20,150	
Depreciation	(W1)	4,000	24,150
Net profit			8,350

Balance sheet as at 31 October 20X1

		£	£
Fixed assets			
Cost	(W1)	20,000	
Less: Depreciation	(W1)	4,000	16,000
Current assets			
Stock	(W6)	7,500	
Debtors	(W4)	15,500	
Cash	(W5)	22,000	
	(W2)	45,000	
Less: Current liabilities	(W2)	30,000	15,000
			31,000
Capital as at 1 November 20X0	(W9)		28,650
Add profit for year			8,350
			37,000
Less: Drawings			6,000
			31,000

Workings

(W1) Fixed assets

Business started 1 November 20X0, so only one year's depreciation has been charged

Fixed assets are therefore:

£4,000 × 100/20 = £20,000

(W2) **Current assets and liabilities**

Working capital is £15,000

Current ratio is 1.5:1

Therefore:

Current assets are £15,000 × 1.5/0.5 = £45,000

Current liabilities are £15,000 × 1.0 /0.5 = £30,000

(W3) **Sales**

Net assets are £16,000 + £15,000 (from W1 and W2)

Net assets to turnover is given as 2.5 times

Therefore sales are £31,000 × 2.5 = £77,500

(W4) **Debtors**

Debtors turnover is 5 times

Therefore debtors are £77,500/5 = £ 15,500

(W5) **Cash at bank**

Acid test ratio is 1.25:1

Therefore cash and debtors = 1.25 times liabilities £30,000

= £37,500

Debtors are £15,500, so cash must be £22,000

(W6) **Stock**

Total current assets are £45,000

Cash and debtors total £37,500, therefore stock must be £7,500

(W7) **Cost of sales**

Stock turnover is 6 times

Cost of sales must therefore be 6 × £7,500 = £45,000

(W8) **Expenses**

26% of sales £77,500 = £20,150

(W9) **Opening capital**

Opening capital is worked backwards from closing capital, which must be £31,000

Opening capital is thus

£31,000 + drawings £6,000 (given) – profit £8,350 = £28,650

ANSWER 29

BOND LTD AND FRASER LTD (PILOT PAPER)

(a)

Ratio	Formulae	Bond Ltd	Fraser Ltd
Profitability ratios			
Gross profit percentage	$\dfrac{\text{Gross profit}}{\text{Sales}} \times 100$	$\dfrac{5{,}950}{23{,}800} \times 100 = 25\%$	$\dfrac{7{,}200}{24{,}000} \times 100 = 30\%$
Net profit percentage	$\dfrac{\text{Net profit}}{\text{Sales}} \times 100$	$\dfrac{3{,}450}{23{,}800} \times 100 = 14\%$	$\dfrac{2{,}400}{24{,}000} \times 100 = 10\%$
Earnings per share	$\dfrac{\text{Net profit after tax}}{\text{No of ordinary shares}}$	$\dfrac{2{,}550}{12{,}000} = 21p$	$\dfrac{1{,}800}{20{,}000} = 9p$
Return on capital employed*	$\dfrac{\text{Net profit after tax}}{\text{Capital employed}}$	$\dfrac{2{,}550}{15{,}625} \times 100 = 16\%$	$\dfrac{1{,}800}{23{,}995} \times 100 = 8\%$
Liquidity ratios			
Current ratio	$\dfrac{\text{Current assets}}{\text{Current liabilities}} : 1$	$\dfrac{2{,}600}{1{,}675} :1 = 1.6:1$	$\dfrac{1{,}800}{805} :1 = 2.2:1$
Acid test ratio	$\dfrac{\text{Current assets} - \text{Stock}}{\text{Current liabilities}}$	$\dfrac{2{,}100}{1{,}675} :1 = 1.3:1$	$\dfrac{600}{805} :1 = 0.7:1$

* Credit will be given for alternative calculations providing workings have been shown.

The ratios above are illustrative of the types of ratios candidates might include in their answer. It is not a comprehensive list.

(b)

Ratio	Bond Ltd	Fraser Ltd	Comment
Gross profit percentage	25%	30%	Fraser Ltd is able to achieve a higher gross profit percentage than Bond Ltd. This may be due to a number of factors, e.g. a more effective purchasing strategy or premium pricing.
Net profit percentage	14%	10%	Bond Ltd has a higher net profit percentage than Fraser Ltd. This suggests that Bond Ltd has tighter control of its administrative, selling and distribution expenses than Fraser Ltd.
Earnings per share	21p	9p	Bond Ltd has a higher EPS than Fraser Ltd. This suggests that Bond Ltd is probably a better investment. However, more information is required on the market value of shares.
Return on capital employed	16%	8%	Bond Ltd's return on capital employed is double that of Fraser Ltd. This suggests that Bond Ltd is managed more efficiently than Fraser Ltd.

Ratio	Bond Ltd	Fraser Ltd	Comment
Current ratio	1.6:1	2.2:1	The current ratio for Bond Ltd looks weaker than Fraser Ltd although both companies appear to have sufficient current assets to cover their current liabilities.
Acid test ratio	1.3:1	0.7:1	Bond Ltd has a higher acid test ratio than Fraser Ltd. It suggests that Fraser Ltd has poorer working capital management as it has very high levels of stock and debtors together with low levels of creditors. One possibility is that it has old or obsolete stock.

There should be some evidence of trying to interpret the ratios, while acknowledging the limitations of the information available. Other comments, if appropriate, will also be given credit.

SAMPLE PAST EXAMINATION PAPER

This Past paper has been included by kind permission of the Institute of Certified Bookkeepers

THE INSTITUTE OF CERTIFIED BOOKKEEPERS

Level III Diploma in Manual Bookkeeping

February 2009

Time allowed: 3 hours

INSTRUCTIONS TO CANDIDATES

Candidates should attempt all five questions

To pass this paper, candidates must achieve a minimum of 60% overall.

Answers should be **written in blue or black ink/ballpoint** and completed in the answer book provided. Please note that any work in pencil will not be marked.

All workings should be shown in the answer book. Scrap paper should not be used.

The use of correcting fluid is not permitted

A single line down the centre of the page is sufficient for ledger ruling. Folio numbers are not required

For cash books and petty cash books, the use of two (facing) pages in the answer book is suggested

Calculators may be used provided that they are battery operated or solar powered, noiseless, non-programmable and do not give a print out.

Whilst in the examination room, all mobile telephones and pagers **MUST** be turned off.

This page intentionally left blank

You are a Certified Bookkeeper and all of the following questions (excluding Q4) are based on work you have recently undertaken on behalf of your clients.

Question 1

You are working on the financial statements of Sandsend Cricket Club for year ended 31 December 2008.

Scenario (1)

The Club runs a bar and the Chairman is concerned that stock has recently been taken from club premises without payment.

He supplies you with the following information for year ended 31 December 2008:

Opening Stock 1 January 2008 £2900, Purchases £45600, Closing Stock   31 December 2008 £3400, Sales £71200.

The club maintains a policy of achieving a 40% gross profit on sales.

Task 1.1

Determine the sales value of stock not accounted for.

Task 1.2

What other financial implications to the club are apparent from these accounts?

Scenario (2)

At 1 January 2008 the subscriptions account showed that there were subscriptions in arrears of £90 and subscriptions in advance of £60.

During the year the treasurer banked £850 in the form of subscriptions and currently there were arrears of £70 and subscriptions paid in advance of £50 at 31 December 2008.

It became apparent during the year that £50 of the opening arrears was not recoverable.

Task 1.3

Write up the subscriptions account for the year showing clearly the transfer of the amount to the club's Income and Expenditure Account and state clearly how you would deal with the arrears that are no longer recoverable.

Scenario (3)

The treasurer keeps an account headed general expenses.

On the 1 January there was an opening accrual of £75 and an opening prepayment of £105.

During the year, items coded general expenses and paid through the bank amounted to £1050 and, at the end of the year, there was a closing accrual of £95 and a closing prepayment of £115.

Task 1.4

Write up the general expenses account for the year, showing clearly the transfer to the Income and Expenditure Account.

Scenario (4)

The Machinery and Equipment Account at cost on 1 January 2008 was £65000 and the accumulated depreciation to date was £39000.

A mower purchased on the 1 January 2005 for £13000 with a useful life of 5 years was sold for £6000 during the year. It is club policy to depreciate this class of assets at 20% per annum straight line; depreciating in the year of purchase but not in the year of sale.

During the year a replacement mower was purchased for £15500.

Task 1.5

Write up the following accounts for the year showing clearly the accounting treatment of the above items:

- Disposal Account
- Machinery and Equipment at Cost
- Depreciation Provision, Machinery and Equipment

Task 1.6

Show an extract from the Balance Sheet at 31 December 2008 showing Machinery and Equipment at Cost, Depreciation to Date, and Net Book Value.

Scenario (5)

The club sells club shirts to members at £12.00 each. These cost the club £7.50. Recently 40 of these items were damaged by a flood at the clubhouse and will be sold at £5 each.

Task 1.7

What value should be placed on these in the closing stock at 31 December 2008 and why?

(Total 20 marks)

Question 2

You are now working on the final accounts of Tony Cook, a sole trader who is not too competent at maintaining his financial records.

You establish that on 1 January 2008 balances were:

	£
Vehicles at Cost	120,000
Equipment at Cost	180,000
Depreciation provision:	
Vehicles	40,000

Equipment	80,000
Sales Ledger Control	210,400
Purchase Ledger Control	165,500
Accruals:	
Telephone	1500
Heat and Light	5100
Pre-payments	
Rent	10,600
Insurance	14,500
Bank	8,000
Stock	80,600

Task 2.1

Prepare an opening Trial Balance to determine the value of Capital.

You also determine the following:

- Bad debts of £50000 had been written off in the year

- Payments from debtors during the year were £1175000 and debtors at 31 December 2008 were £245500

- During the year Tony had withdrawn £95100 for personal use

- Stock valuation at 31 December 2008 was £175500

- Payments to suppliers had been £710000 and creditors at 31 December 2008 was £165000

- Prepayment as at 31 December 2008 was: Rent £11600

- Accruals as at 31 December 2008: Heat and Light £5750, Telephone £1100
  Bank payments in the year were:

	£
Insurance	28200
Rent	39500
Rates	5100
Heat and Light	32200
Telephone	12500
Motor Vehicle Running Costs	18750
Wages	126500

Depreciation

Vehicles are depreciated at 25% of their original value and equipment at 20% on Net Book Value.

(4 marks)

Task 2.2

Prepare the following financial statements for Tony Cook:

- Trading and Profit and Loss Account for year ended 31 December 2008
- Balance sheet as at that date

(16 marks)

(Total 20 marks)

Question 3

You have recently been advising a partnership for Karl and Ernie Hayes who are considering admitting a new partner, Barry Hayes, on the 1 January 2009. The profit for the year ended 31 December 2008, had been £112500 and the following additional detail is available:

Capital Accounts 1/1/08

| E Hayes | £160000 |
| K Hayes | £145000 |

Current Accounts 1/1/08

| E Hayes | £16500 CR |
| K Hayes | £21400 CR |

Partners are allowed 6% on capital at the start of the year and are charged 4% on drawings.

Drawings during the year had been:

| E Hayes | £25100 |
| K Hayes | £21200 |

and partners are to be credited with the following salaries:

| E Hayes | £20000 |
| K Hayes | £15500 |

Profits to be shared equally

Task 3.1

Prepare the partnership appropriation account for year ended 31 December 2008.

(6 marks)

Task 3.2

Prepare the partners' current accounts showing clearly the balances as at 31 December 2008.

(6 marks)

Admission of a Partner

On the 1 January Barry is admitted to the partnership and it is agreed that:

- He will contribute £60000 in the form of a cheque
- Land and Buildings currently valued in the accounts at £125000 are to be revalued to £165000
- It is agreed that goodwill will be valued at £80000 but this intangible asset will not be kept in the books of the partnership

Profits to be shared 40% - E. Hayes, 40% - K Hayes, 20% - B Hayes.

Task 3.3

Prepare the Capital Accounts of the Partners following the admission of Barry, showing clearly the treatment of the revaluation of the assets and the goodwill.

(8 marks)

(Total 20 marks)

Question 4

Please complete the following statements.

Write the **answers in your answer booklet.**
(There is no need to rewrite the complete sentence.)

PED Ltd had the following balances in its accounts at 31 December 2008.

Land and Buildings £1.2m; Plant and Equipment £0.75m; Debtors £0.5m; Stocks £0.25m; Bank £0.15m; Creditors £0.7m; Long Term Liabilities (Loans) £0.95m.

1   What is the value of Equity or Shareholders' Interest?

2   What is the value of Capital Employed?

3   What is the value of Total Assets?

4   What is the value of Total Liabilities?

5   What is the value of Net Current Assets?

6   Gearing is a measure of long term liabilities to capital employed, is this company therefore high or low geared?

7   If the company decided to issue a further 200000 shares (£1 each nominal) at £1.40, the total assets of the company would increase to what?

8   The above transaction would involve a DR to Bank and a CR for what value, and to which accounts in the company's books?

9   The relationship of Current Assets to Current Liabilities is a measure of what?

10   In the data for (1) above if profits for year had been £0.58m what was the Return on Capital Employed?

(Total 20 marks)

Question 5

Your assistant has been working on the final accounts for Sandsend Engineering Ltd and has prepared the following Trial Balance after preparing the Profit and Loss account for year ended 31 December 2008:

	DR	CR
Premises	250000	
Equipment	190000	
Motor Vehicles	52000	
Provision for Depreciation:		
Premises		55000
Equipment		118750
Motor Vehicles		31200
Stocks	49500	
Debtors	37500	
Prepayments	2500	
Bank	19250	
Creditors		21600
Accruals		5750
Long Term Loan		40000
Share Capital		180000
Revenue Reserve (profit bfwd 1/1/08)		53350
Profit for year		95100
	£600750	£600750

You examine the file and find that additional information is available and no entries have yet been made through the books for these items:

- A bad debt of £4500 has to be written off

- A provision for doubtful debts of 4% is to be provided on the remaining debtors

- A piece of equipment that originally cost £40000 in year ending 31 December 2005 had been sold on 31 December 2008 for £12000 and a cheque has been received. Equipment is depreciated at 25% straight line method

- Further accruals and pre-payments need to be accounted for as:

    Accrual : Heat, Light and Power £1300
    Prepayment : Insurance £950

- 6 months interest at 6% per annum needs to be provided for on the loan

- Stock items have been damaged. This stock had an original cost of £2100 and normally sold for £2940, but now has a saleable value of £1540

- It was decided to revalue the premises to £300000

Task 5.1

Prepare a schedule to show the effect of the above items on the profit for year.

(10 marks)

Task 5.2

Prepare the Balance Sheet of Sandsend Engineering Ltd as at 31 December 2008 having accounted for the items above.

(10 marks)

(Total 20 marks)

LEVEL III DIPLOMA IN MANUAL BOOKKEEPING

February 2009

Suggested Answers

Q1

Sandsend Cricket Club

Task 1.1

Cost of Sales:

Opening stock	2900
Purchases	45600
	48500
Less closing stock	3400
	45100

This should represent 60% of sales therefore sales should have been £<u>75167</u>

Sales value of stock not accounted for £3967

Task 1.2

The club must be registered for VAT as their sales are above the registration limit; therefore VAT on this discrepancy must be accounted for.

Task 1.3

Subscriptions a/c

1 Jan	Balance b/d	90.00	1 Jan	Balance b/d		60.00
31 Dec	Balance c/d	50.00	31 Dec	Bank		850.00
31 Dec	I&E a/c	890.00	31 Dec	Balance c/d		70.00
			31 Dec	I&E a/c Sub w/o		50.00
		1030.00				1030.00
1 Jan	Balance b/d	70.00	1 Jan	Balance b/d		50.00

The £50 is simply written off as a debt.

Task 1.4

General Expenses Account

1 Jan	Balance b/d	105.00	1 Jan	Balance b/d	75.00
31 Dec	Bank	1050.00	31 Dec	Balance c/d	115.00
31 Dec	Balance c/d	95.00	31 Dec	I&E	1060.00
		1250.00			1250.00

Task 1.5

Disposal Account

31 Dec	Machinery and Equipment	13000.00	31 Dec	Dep'n Provision	7800.00
31 Dec	Profit on Disposal	800.00	31 Dec	Bank	6000.00
		13800.00			13800.00

Machinery and Equipment

1 Jan	Balance b/d	65000.00	31 Dec	Disposal a/c	13000.00
31 Dec	Bank	15500.00	31 Dec	Balance c/d	67500.00
		80500.00			80500.00
1 Jan	Balance b/d	67500.00			

Depreciation Provision (Machinery and Equipment)

31 Dec	Disposal a/c	7800.00	1 Jan	Balance b/d	39000.00
31 Dec	Balance c/d	44700.00	31 Dec	I&E a/c	13500.00
		52500.00			52500.00
			1 Jan	Balance b/d	44700.00

Task 1.6

Balance Sheet Extract

	Cost	Dep'n	NBV
Machinery and Equipment	67500	44700	22800

Task 1.7

Original cost 40 @ £7.50 £300

Revised cost 40 @ £5.00 £200

Stock should be valued at the lower of cost or net realisable value therefore included in stock valuation at £200.

Q1 Total 20 Marks

Q2

Task 2.1

Working Papers

Sales:

Sales Ledger Control

1 Jan	Balance b/d	210400	31 Dec	Bad Debts	50000
31 Dec	Sales	1260100	31 Dec	Bank	1175000
			31 Dec	Balance c/d	245500
		1470500			1470500

Sales   £1260100

Purchases:

Purchase Ledger Control

31 Dec	Bank	710000	1 Jan	Balance b/d	165500
31 Dec	Balance c/d	165000	31 Dec	Purchases	709500
		875000			875000

Purchases   £709500

Expenses:

Telephone		HLP		Rent		Insurance	
12500	1500	32200	5100	10600	11600	14500	
1100	12100	5750	32850	39500	38500	28200	42700
13600	13600	37950	37950	50100	50100	42700	42700

Rates	£5100
MVRC	£18750
Wages	£126500
Bad debts w/o	£50000
Dep'n	£30000 Motor Vehicles
	£20000 Equipment

KAPLAN PUBLISHING

Task 2.1

Trial Balance as at 1 January 2008

	DR	CR
Vehicles at Cost	120000	
Equipment at Cost	180000	
Dep'n Provisions MV		40000
Dep'n Provisions Eq		80000
Sales Ledger Control	210400	
Purchase Ledger Control		165500
Accruals		6600
Pre-payments	25100	
Bank	8000	
Stock	80600	
Capital		332000
	624100	624100

Total 2.1   4 marks

Task 2.2

Trading and Profit and Loss Account for year ended 31 December 2008

	£	£
Sales		1260100
Opening Stock	80600	
Add Purchases	709500	
	790100	
Less Stock 31 December 2008	175500	
Cost of Sales		614600
Gross Profit		645500
Expenses:		
Telephone	12100	
HLP	32850	
Rent	38500	
Insurance	42700	
Rates	5100	
MVRC	18750	
Wages	126500	
Bad Debts w/o	50000	
Dep'n Motor Vehicles	30000	
Dep'n Equipment	20000	
		376500
Net profit for year		£269000

Balance Sheet as at 31 December 2008

Fixed Assets

	Cost	Dep'n	NBV
Motor Vehicles	120000	70000	50000
Equipment	180000	100000	80000
			130000

Current Assets
Stock   175500
Debtors   245500
Pre-payments   11600
Bank   115150
                                    547750

Less Current Liabilities
Creditors   165000
Accruals   6850
                                    171850

Net Current Assets   375900
Net Assets   £505900

Financed by:
Capital   332000
Add Profit for Year   269000
                                    601000
Less Drawings   95100
                                                   £505900

Total 2.2 16 marks

Q2 Total 20 marks

Q3

Task 3.1

Appropriation Account for year ended 31 December 2008

	£	£
Profit for year		112500
Interest on Drawings:		
EH	1004	
KH	848	
		1852
		114352
Interest on Capital:		
EH	9600	
KH	8700	
		18300
		96052
Salaries:		
EH	20000	
KH	15500	
		35500
		60552
Share of profit EH	30276	
KH	30276	
		60552

6 marks

Task 3.2

Partners' Current Accounts

		EH	KH			EH	KH
31/12	Interest on Drawings	1004	848	1/1/09	Balance b/d	16500	21400
31/12	Drawings	25100	21200	31/12	Interest on Capital	9600	8700
31/12	Balance c/d	50272	53828	31/12	Salaries	20000	15500
				31/12	Share of Profit	30276	30276
		76376	75876			76376	75876
				1/1/09	Balance b/d	50272	53828

6 marks

Task 3.3

Partners' Capital Accounts

		EH	KH	BH			EH	KH	BH
1/1/09	Goodwill	32000	32000	16000	1/1/09	Balance b/d	160000	145000	
1/1/09	Balance c/d	188000	173000	44000	1/1/09	Bank			60000
					1/1/09	Revaluation	20000	20000	
					1/1/09	Goodwill	40000	40000	
		220000	205000	60000			220000	205000	60000
					1/1/09	Balance b/d	188000	173000	44000

8 marks

KAPLAN PUBLISHING

Q4

1	£1.2m
2	£2.15m
3	£2.85m
4	£1.65m
5	£0.20m
6	High
7	£280000
8	CR Capital £200000 CR Share Premium £80000
9	Liquidity
10	26.9%
	Going Concern

Q4 Total 20 marks

Q5
Task 5.1

	£	
Profit for year	95100	
Bad debt	(4500)	Take out of debtors
Bad debt provision	(1320)	- " -

```
      Disposal a/c
  40000  | Dep'n  30000                Bank + 12000
         | Bank   12000    2000        EQ – 40000
                                       Dep'n - 30000
```

Accruals	(1300)	Balance Sheet
Pre-payments	950	
Interest accrued	(1200)	Accrual BS
Stock adjustment	(560)	Adjust stock
Premises revaluation	-	Reval Res + 165000 Premises + 165
Revised Profit	£89170	

10 marks

Task 5.2

Balance Sheet of Sandsend Engineering Ltd as at 31 December 2008

Fixed Assets	**Cost**	**Dep'n**	**NBV**
Premises	300000		300000
Equipment	150000	88750	61250
Motor Vehicles	52000	31200	20800
			382050

Current Assets			
Stocks		48940	
Debtors Less Provision		31680	
Pre-payments		3450	
Bank		31250	
		115320	

Less Current Liabilities			
Creditors		21600	
Accruals		8250	
		29850	

Net Current Assets		85470
Total Assets Less Current Liabilities		467520
Less Long Term Liability		
Loan		40000
Net Assets		£427520

Financed by:

Capital and Reserves		
Capital	180000	
Revaluation Reserve	105000	
Revenue Reserve	142520	
		£427520

10 marks

Q5 Total 20 marks